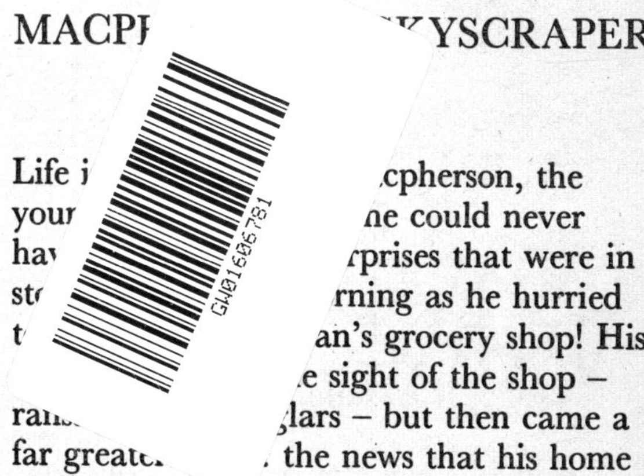

MACPH… …KYSCRAPER

Life i… …cpherson, the your… …he could never hav… …rprises that were in st… …rning as he hurried t… …an's grocery shop! His … …e sight of the shop – ran… …glars – but then came a far great… … the news that his home was to be pulled down . . .

MACPHERSON'S SKYSCRAPER was chosen as a Children's Book of the Year in 1978.

Jacket illustration by Val Biro

ABOUT THE AUTHOR

Lavinia Derwent was born in No-Man's-Land on a farm on the Scottish side of the Border, so remote that she knew more animals than human-beings. Her head being full of 'beasts', she made up stories about them, invented a character called TAMMY TROOT and later an island called SULA, full of seals and sea-birds.

When she came to live in the big city of Glasgow she met many human-beings, but none that interested her more than a cheerful boy whom she saw in the street, lugging a heavy message-basket. MACPHERSON! Since then Macpherson has taken the place of 'beasts' in her head. Through him she has had many exciting adventures; and is delighted that so many children also follow his fortunes, sending her letters and drawings about Macpherson, Maisie and the other characters.

Macpherson's Skyscraper

Lavinia Derwent

Illustrated by Lesley Smith

KNIGHT BOOKS
Hodder and Stoughton

First published by Burke Publishing

This edition first published by Blackie & Son Ltd. 1978

Knight Books edition 1980

The characters and situations in this book are entirely imaginary and bear no relation to any real person or actual happening

Printed and bound in Great Britain for Hodder and Stoughton Paperbacks, a division of Hodder and Stoughton Ltd., Mill Road, Dunton Green, Sevenoaks, Kent (Editorial Office: 47 Bedford Square, London, WC1 3DP) by Richard Clay (The Chaucer Press) Ltd, Bungay, Suffolk

ISBN 0 340 24038 5

By the same author:

Macpherson's Lighthouse Adventure

Contents

I

A Day of Surprises

"Hi, you! Where d'you think you're going?"

Macpherson skidded to a standstill, and stared up at the policeman who was barring his way. It was not his friend, the Highland bobby. This was a big, black-browed man with no nonsense about him.

Macpherson had been helter-skeltering along the street, trying to reach the grocer's shop in time. Old Skinflint—whose real name was Mr McGlashan—would have plenty to say to him if he was late.

"Message-boys!" he would say. "They're perfect pests! I've a good mind to flay you alive! Get on with your work before I lose my temper...."

But today Old Skinflint took no notice of Macpherson. He was standing at the shop door, beside the policeman, with a lost look on his face.

"What's happened?" asked Macpherson in surprise.

"Can you not see?"

Macpherson gaped at the broken window and gasped, "Mercy me!" Inside, everything was topsy-turvy. The tins of soup and fruit salad, which Macpherson had helped to build into a neat pyramid, lay jumbled up in an untidy heap. The notices advertising HOME-CURED BACON and FRESH EGGS were knocked flat. A brick lay beside them.

"Goodness gracious!" cried Macpherson. "Was it a smash-and-grab?"

Nobody bothered to answer him. Nobody except Miss Peacock, the kind-faced assistant. She was at the door, still wearing her hat, and looking paler than usual.

"They blew the safe," she told Macpherson, in a shocked voice.

"Goodness gracious!" No wonder Old Skinflint had such a stricken look on his face. It was the worst thing that could have happened to him, losing his money. "Did they get anything?" asked Macpherson.

Miss Peacock nodded. Just then an exciting sound was heard—the sound of a police car rushing to the scene.

"Oh my!" cried Macpherson, "we're fairly in the thick of it! Wait till Grandpa hears about this!"

"You keep out of the way!" said the policeman, gruffly. "Get into the shop and don't touch a thing."

The shop was at sixes and sevens. It would take days to put it right again, if not weeks. Everything had been pushed off the shelves and flung on to the floor. Eggs, butter, cheese, sugar—all were mixed up with sauce-bottles, oatmeal, and packets of soap powder. Even the weighing-machine had been thrown off the counter.

"You should see the back-shop," whispered Miss Peacock. "They've blown a hole in the ceiling."

"Never!" This was something Macpherson must see! But another policeman was guarding the door to the back-shop.

"Keep out!" he ordered, "and don't put your hands on anything."

"Fingerprints," explained Miss Peacock. She and Macpherson stood in the middle of the wreckage, not knowing what to do to help.

The grocer came in followed by two men in raincoats. Detectives! Their keen eyes seemed to look through everybody and everything like x-rays. Macpherson felt uneasy in their presence, almost as if *he* had done the deed himself.

The grocer was arguing with them. "Can't waste any more time hanging about. All I want is to get the shop cleared up as quickly as possible and put a BUSINESS AS USUAL sign in the window. Otherwise, I'll be ruined. Ruined!"

Macpherson was sorry for him, though he knew it would take more than a burglary to ruin Old Skinflint, and him with so much money in the bank.

"The insurance will cover your losses," one of the detectives told him. "I'm afraid you'll have to shut the shop for the day, Mr McGlashan."

"Shut the shop!" burst out Old Skinflint. "I'll lose all my customers! I'll be ruined!"

"Is there anything I can do, Mr McGlashan,

sir?" asked Macpherson, anxious to help.

"Yes! Clear out of my way!" said the grocer impatiently. "Off you go!"

"You mean I can go home?"

"You can go to the moon, for all I care! But be sure to be here early tomorrow. You'll need to work twice as hard to make up for it. If not thrice!"

"Oh yes, I will! Thank you, Mr McGlashan, sir."

Anything to get away, so that he could rush home and tell the tale to Grandpa. It would have been fun to stay, of course, and have his finger-prints taken and watch the detectives at work. But a holiday was even better. He said "Cheerio" to Miss Peacock, and pushed past the policeman at the door.

"Watch it, you!" The man looked at him suspiciously. "Let's see what you've got in your pockets."

"Me?" Surely the man did not suspect him of being the thief! Macpherson felt in his pockets, just in case the contents of the safe had found their way in. No! not a single coin.

"What's that?" asked the policeman, bending down to look.

"A catapult," said Macpherson, pulling it out.

"Breaking windows, I expect!"

"No, no. I haven't!" protested Macpherson.

"Well, watch yourself! Away you go!"

Macpherson wasted no time. He sped away down the street, breaking his own record in his hurry to get home. He did not hear the roar of the traffic, or the hooting of the boats on the great River Clyde. He could only hear himself telling the story to Grandpa. "Fancy, Grandpa! A smash-and-grab raid . . . !"

"Look out!"

Macpherson was about to whip round the corner into the street that led home to Clyde-View Tenements when he heard the noise. *Crash!* He ducked his head as the whole side of a building came toppling down into the street. A thick cloud of dust rose up into the air. A chimney smashed on to the pavement. Bricks flew in all directions; and a moment later nothing was left of the building but a heap of rubble.

"Mercy me!" Macpherson rubbed the dust out of his eyes and stared at the gap which had once been a block of flats. What had happened to all the people who had lived there? Where on earth had they gone? He could see bits of flowery wallpaper still stuck to the side of the gaping wall, and a fireplace round which a family had once gathered. Had the people found a new fireplace and a new home?

The workmen had stopped for a breather, and were sitting amongst the rubble. Some were reading their newspapers; others were eating sandwiches from a paper bag.

"What's going on?" asked Macpherson, still feeling dazed.

One of the men raised his eyebrows and gave him a comical look. "See for yourself, chum! We're fishing for elephants!"

Macpherson's face flushed. "I mean, why are you pulling the house down?"

"Search me, chum!" The man took a bite of bread-and-cheese. "We're just obeying orders."

Macpherson was not satisfied. He looked around at the debris and asked, "But what about the people who lived there?"

The man's eyebrows twitched. "Oh, we play fair, chum! We give them a sporting chance to get out first!"

Macpherson could see it was no use asking *him*. All the same, he tried again. "Where on earth do they go?"

"Buckingham Palace, I expect! Look, chum, where they go is their business. Ours is to pull down the houses." He pointed in the direction of Macpherson's own street, seen through the gap. "That lot's coming down, too, and high time, if you ask me. Otherwise it'll tumble down on its own."

"What?"

Macpherson was so stunned that he almost tumbled down himself. "You—you don't mean Clyde-View Tenements?"

"That's right chum!" The man went on munching his bread-and-cheese. What did *he* care? It was only another heap of stones. But to Macpherson it was home.

Home!—the place he knew best in the world; the place where he and Grandpa and Aunt Janet had always lived. How often had he helped the old man to climb the worn stairs! How often had he played in the tumble-down coal-cellar in the back-court! How often had he run home, knowing that Grandpa would be there, watching and waiting for him at the window!

Macpherson's heart sank when he thought of the old man and how much he loved the view from the window. Day after day he sat there, working at his ships-in-bottles and looking out at the real ships on the river. Where would he sit now, and what would happen to them all, when their home lay in ruins?

Macpherson tried to swallow the lump in his throat. He had thought everything would go on for ever in the same happy-go-lucky way. Now his whole world had fallen down, just like the old buildings.

He pulled himself up. Perhaps it was a mistake. Maybe a miracle would happen and everything would be the same as before. Macpherson was a great believer in miracles. He had only to summon his slaves and they would obey his commands.

"What is thy wish, O Master?"

"I wish Clyde-View Tenements to stay up for ever and ever."

"*Cheep-cheep!*" It was not his slaves who answered but a small bird fluttering amongst the rubble as if looking for somewhere to settle.

"What's that?" said Macpherson, forgetting his own troubles for the moment.

"If you ask me, chum, it's a budgie. Lost, like enough!" The man stood up, throwing away his empty paper bag. "That's nothing to what I've seen, when the houses come down. Stray dogs and cats and rabbits and hamsters and even goldfish . . . ."

"Bonnie boy! Joey's a bonnie wee boy! A bonnie wee boy!" The budgerigar fluttered its wings and then flew towards Macpherson. "How d'you do? Joey's a bonnie wee boy . . . ."

Macpherson held out his hand and the bird landed safely on it. The boy held it gently, saying, "It's okay, Joey! You're safe!" Then he turned to the man and said, "I wonder whose it is? How could I find out? Maybe someone's looking for it."

"Not them! If you ask me, chum, somebody wants to be rid of it. You'd better do the same."

"Oh no!" said Macpherson, holding it closer. Poor homeless little thing! *He* would soon be the same himself. "I'm going to keep it."

"Oh well, that's up to you!"

It was up to him all right! Where could he keep it? It was no use trying to smuggle it into the house. Grandpa would welcome it, of course; but Aunt Janet would chase him for his life. He could hear her scolding voice: "Take that nasty beast away!" (All animals and birds were "nasty beasts" to Aunt Janet.) "I have enough bother cleaning up after you and your Grandpa without bothering with pests like that."

All the same, he was going to keep it. There was the old coal-cellar in the back-court where he had kept many a forbidden thing in his day. Davy Jones' locker, Grandpa called it. He could hide it there till he thought of a better place. "Come on, Joey! We're going home!"

Grandpa was at the window as usual, with his head bowed over his work. He was busy making a model of the *Hebridean*, one of the sturdy ships that sailed to the small islands scattered around Scotland. The old man, not expecting Macpherson home so soon, was too absorbed to look up.

The boy watched him from a distance. Poor Grandpa! Little did he know there would soon be no window to work at and that, before long, his whole world would come tumbling down.

"Yoo-hoo, Macpherthon!"

Wee Maisie Murphy came shuffling towards him in a pair of her mother's bedroom-slippers, several sizes too big for her. Now and again she stepped out of one of them and had to go back to get it. But Maisie did not mind. She was used to wearing misfits. There were far too many Murphies for them all to have new clothes.

Maisie made up for it by decking herself out in any finery she could find. Today she was dressed as a bride, with an old lace curtain trailing from her head and a bunch of plastic flowers in her hand.

"Thee me, Macpherthon!" She whirled round in front of him, losing a slipper in the process. "What do I look like?"

"Daft!" said Macpherson bluntly.

"I do not! I look great! Tho there!"

The bride's lip began to quiver and a tear trickled down her chubby cheek. She was a great one, was Maisie, for weeping one moment and laughing the next.

"Okay, you look great!" said Macpherson hastily. He had too many things on his mind to waste time arguing with a lassie.

Maisie's tears dried like magic as she heard a faint *cheep-cheep*. "What'th that you've got in your hand, Macpherthon? Oh my! it'th a wee bird! Ith it a canary, like the one we had?"

"No, it's a budgie." The mention of the canary had given Macpherson an idea. "I say, Maisie, maybe you can help me."

"Oh yeth, I will, Macpherthon! What'll I do?"

"You remember when the canary died...?"

"Poor wee Bobby!" Maisie's tears had begun to flow again. "He'th buried in the back-court, poor wee thing."

"Have you still got his cage?"

"Yeth, I think tho," gulped Maisie.

"Do you think I could have a loan of it?"

"Thertainly, if I can find it."

When it came to it, Maisie was practical enough, especially when she could do something to help her hero. Without more ado, she went slip-slopping away into the house, stepping over the twins who were sitting sucking their thumbs on the doorstep.

The latest baby, bouncing about in the shabby pram, let out a wail to attract her attention. But Maisie only said, "Keep quiet, you!" and went about her business.

There were so many things in Macpherson's mind that he did not know which to think about first as he waited for Maisie to come back. The smash-and-grab raid! The pulling down of the tenements! The budgie! Too much had happened in one short day.

The twins got up together from the doorstep and came tottering over to him. They stood before him, staring hopefully at his pockets. Macpherson knew what they wanted! "No! Sorry! No sweets today. See! Watch the wee bird."

The budgie obliged by saying his piece. "How d'you do? Joey's a bonnie wee boy! A bonnie wee boy!"

The twins began to chuckle and stretch out their hands towards the bird. They were learning to speak themselves, but were not as far advanced as the budgie. "Wee boy! Bonnie wee boy!" they tried to imitate him.

The bride came hurrying out of the house, tripping over her veil. She had a look of triumph on her face, and was carrying an empty bird-cage in place of her bouquet.

"Here it ith, Macpherthon! I've found it! Good for me!" Maisie was always ready to pat her own back. "Thee! There'th plenty of theed left in it."

There was also a bell and a ladder and a swing and a little looking-glass. The budgie was not going to lack home comforts!

"Thanks a lot, Maisie," said Macpherson

gratefully. "Come on, Joey! In you go!"

The twins clapped their hands when they saw the budgie fluttering into the cage. He took one look round his new home and settled down on the swing. All was well—except that he must be kept out of Aunt Janet's sight, at all costs.

"I'm going to hide him in the coal-cellar, and you're not to tell, Maisie. You understand?"

"Yeth, I understand." Knowing Aunt Janet, Maisie understood only too well. "Come on, you two," she said to the twins, and took hold of their sticky hands. "Leave Macpherthon alone. He'th got thingth to do."

Macpherson went away carrying the bird-cage and thinking Maisie wasn't so bad, after all. For a lassie! If only Aunt Janet was as understanding! He looked up at the window, afraid she might be watching; but only Grandpa was there, still bent over his work.

Macpherson hurried through to the back-court and put out a hand to open the coal-cellar door. The next moment he leapt back in dismay as a tall figure emerged with a pail in her hand.

"Aunt Janet! Oh d-dear! I'm in the s-soup!"

2

Breaking the News

There was something strange about Aunt Janet today. She did not seem to notice the bird-cage. Indeed, she scarcely noticed Macpherson. But *he* noticed something about her. She had been crying!

Never in all his life had Macpherson known such a thing to happen. Aunt Janet never showed her feelings—except her anger—and she showed *that* often enough. Unlike Maisie Murphy, she never gave way to laughter or tears. Never except today! There was no doubt about it; her eyes were red-rimmed, her cheeks were still wet, and she was biting her lips to keep them from trembling.

"Wh-what's the matter, Aunt Janet?" Macpherson would sooner have had her scolding him than looking like that. "Is—is anything wrong?"

Aunt Janet looked at him without seeming to see him. It gave him cold shivers down his spine. Had something terrible happened to Grandpa? Yet he had seen the old man only a moment ago at the window.

"We're to be shifted!" gulped Aunt Janet.

"Shifted?"

"Moved! They're going to pull down Clyde-View Tenements!"

Macpherson could not help feeling relieved. It was terrible, of course, but he had feared something even worse. In any case, he had already had time to recover from the first shock. But Aunt Janet, it seemed, would never get over it. For once she found it difficult to keep a tight rein on herself.

"I could kill them!" she burst out. "Pulling down *our* house! After all those years! Where will we go? What will we do? It's a disgrace! A perfect disgrace!"

Macpherson did not know what to do or say to comfort her. He tried to put out a hand to touch hers, but she thrust him away. "You're not to tell him, mind!" she said fiercely.

"Who? Grandpa? No, I won't tell him."

It was the first time they had ever shared a secret, these two. He and Grandpa had hundreds, if not thousands; but it was strange to be on such close terms with someone as stern as Aunt Janet.

"It'll break his heart!" she cried, wiping away her tears with the back of her hand. "I can't bear to think of it! It'll be the death of him!"

"Oh, Aunt Janet!"

It was awful to see her in such a state. Macpherson was learning a lot of things about her; that her heart was soft, in spite of all her scoldings; that she loved her shabby home; and that Grandpa was more important to her than anything else in the world.

Macpherson longed to show her that he understood. "Let me take the coal-pail, Aunt Janet," he began, when a small voice broke in: "Tweet-tweet! Joey's a bonnie wee boy!"

Macpherson gave a guilty start. He had forgotten about the budgie, even though he was still holding the bird-cage in his hand. No use trying to hide it from Aunt Janet.

"It's—it's a wee bird," he told her. "It's lost! I thought I might give it a home."

"In the coal-cellar!" said Aunt Janet, looking at the budgie for the first time. "That's not much of a home."

Macpherson's heart beat faster. "You mean, I could maybe keep it in the house?"

Aunt Janet did not say "Yes". On the other hand, she did not say "No".

She only picked up the coal-pail and strode away, reminding him, "You're not to tell your Grandpa."

"No, I won't, Aunt Janet!"

Macpherson followed her, carrying the cage. It was a great victory for him. How happy it would have made him, had it not been for the terrible secret he and Aunt Janet were sharing. As he went up the stone stairs behind her, he noticed for the first time how worn they were. The walls were dirty, the windows on each landing were broken, and the paint was peeling off every doorway. There was no doubt about it, the building was ready to tumble down of its own accord. Yet, it was home, and Macpherson loved every shabby inch of it.

"Ho-ro! Up she rises!"

As they reached the top of the stairs they could hear Grandpa singing one of his favourite sea-shanties. "Is that you, Janet woman?" he said, as she opened the door. Then his old eyes lit up when he caught sight of Macpherson. "Ship ahoy! I didn't expect you back so soon, Macpherson, my boy. Come on; tell me everything!"

Aunt Janet gave Macpherson a warning look and left the two of them together. There was so much to tell that the boy did not know where to begin. He blurted out his story about the burglary and the budgie, but he kept back the main thing that was on his mind. All the same, he had an uneasy feeling that Grandpa knew there was something else.

"Heave ho! What a day *you*'ve had, my hearty! Everything happens to Macpherson!" chuckled the old man. "Is that the lot?"

"Y-yes, that's the lot, Grandpa." Macpherson did not look him straight in the eye. He had never told the old man a lie before; but surely this was in a good cause. He turned to the budgie, trying to cover up his confusion. "See, Grandpa, his name's Joey, and he's a bonnie wee bird."

"A bonnie wee bird," repeated Joey, while Grandpa cried, "Good for you, Macpherson, my boy! I've always wanted a shipmate like him. He'll be great company for me when you're out. I can hang him up here in the window, and the two of us can talk away, while I'm working. You wait! I'll have him singing sea-shanties before you can shiver your timbers!"

Grandpa looked over his shoulder to see if Aunt Janet was listening, and leaned closer to Macpherson. "How did you get round her? I'm surprised she let you keep him."

"Me, too!" said Macpherson, uneasily.

"What are you two whispering about?" asked Aunt Janet, giving Macpherson a severe look.

"Just about the budgie, Aunt Janet," said Macpherson as he helped the old man to hang the cage on a hook in the window.

The bird began to twitter, as if he was happily settled for life.

"Ay! you're not so bad, after all, Janet woman," said Grandpa, twinkling his eyes at her.

"Tuts!" said Aunt Janet, her face flushing. "Clear up your mess! I'm going to make the tea."

It was a high tea, as if they were celebrating something. Aunt Janet cooked a kipper for each of them, and put scones, pancakes, gingerbread and even strawberry jam on the table.

"Splice the mainbrace!" cried Grandpa, smacking his lips. "A feast! Is it somebody's birthday?"

Aunt Janet avoided Macpherson's gaze and said sharply, "No, it's not! Get on with your tea and don't ask silly questions." She always spoke to Grandpa as if he were a naughty child; but Macpherson knew it was only to hide her real feelings.

He would have enjoyed the kipper better if only the secret had not weighed so heavily on his mind. How many more meals would they have in this shabby old kitchen? How would Grandpa take the news when he heard? They could not keep it from him for ever. Would he really break his heart, as Aunt Janet feared?

Macpherson's appetite was gone. He sat back

and looked at the old man, thinking he had never seen him so well or so happy. All the same, Grandpa was too frail to understand the changes that were in store for him. Macpherson dreaded the moment when he must be told.

"Eat up, Macpherson! Have a pancake and some strawberry jam!"

Macpherson shook his head. "I—I'm not hungry, Grandpa!"

The old man was the only one who was eating a hearty meal. Aunt Janet had picked at her kipper and was now sipping her tea. There was a faraway look in her eyes, and now and then she glanced at Macpherson, as if to say, "Don't you dare tell him!"

"What's gone wrong with the pair of you—not eating? Oh well, there's all the more for me," said Grandpa, helping himself.

He was passing his cup for more tea when there was a rattle at the door. Aunt Janet clicked her tongue and said crossly, "If that's wee Maisie Murphy, you can send her packing. She'll have smelt the kippers, likely! Little pest!"

"Och, let the lassie in, Janet woman. She's harmless," said Grandpa mildly. "If it *is* her! Who knows? It might be Her Majesty come to give me a knighthood! Arise, Sir Grandpa!"

The gayer he was, the sadder Aunt Janet and

Macpherson became, knowing how soon his happiness must end. All the same, to humour him, Aunt Janet gave the signal to Macpherson to open the door.

It was Maisie Murphy all right, but she had too much on her mind to bother about kippers. She had taken off her wedding-veil and lost one of her slippers on the way up. But she had not forgotten what she had come to say. No sooner was she inside the door than she blurted out her news.

"I thay! D'you know what, Macpherthon! We're to be knocked down!"

Aunt Janet gave Maisie a look that might have knocked *her* down, there and then.

"Knocked down!" cried Grandpa, in an amused voice. "Who would dare knock you down, Maisie Murphy? Come on, my lass, tell us all about it."

Macpherson's face had gone as white as a sheet. "Stop talking nonsense!" Aunt Janet hissed at Maisie, fiercely.

"It'th not nonthenthe! It'th true! Tho there!" She looked up at Grandpa, seeing that he was the only one who seemed interested in her story. "The whole Tenement'th going to be pulled down. We've all got to move out. Fanthy that!"

For a second there was a stunned silence. Macpherson could hear his own heart thumping—*bump-bump-bump*—and missing a beat now and again. As for Aunt Janet, her face crumpled up as if it was falling to pieces. "I could kill you, Maisie Murphy!" she burst out, and buried her face in her hands.

Maisie stood stock-still, wondering what on earth was the matter with them all. For once she was silenced.

Macpherson hardly dared look at Grandpa to see how he had taken the news. "Oh, please!" he said to his unseen slaves, "don't let him get ill or have a heart-attack."

He was amazed beyond measure to hear the old man give a chuckle. He looked up to see that Grandpa was calmly cutting himself a slice of gingerbread.

"Heave ho, my hearties! I'm glad somebody's spoken about it at last! No use keeping secrets from the old man; eh, Macpherson?" He gave the boy a straight look.

"Oh, Grandpa! You knew!"

Grandpa nodded. "I knew! I've known for days! I was trying to keep it from you and Janet. I thought you might take it badly."

"Badly!" burst out Aunt Janet. Her face was all blotchy by now. She had gone through so many emotions in the last few minutes—from anger to relief, and now back to anger again—that she did not know what to feel. She looked as if she might burst into laughter and tears at the same time. "Where d'you think we're all going to live?"

"In a wigwam!" Grandpa said the first thing that came into his head. "Or maybe Joey'll let us in beside him! What does it matter, Janet woman? We'll all be together."

Aunt Janet gave a sniff and a snort and a gulp, but no words came out. All that Macpherson could say was, "Oh, Grandpa!" The relief was so great that he, too, did not know whether to laugh or cry. Grandpa understood, and gave the boy a wink, while Maisie shuffled her one slipper and got back into the conversation.

"I thay! I've got more to tell you, Macpherthon! We won't need to live in a wagwam."

"Wigwam!" corrected Macpherson. "Why not?"

"Becauthe," Maisie took a deep breath. "Becauthe we're all going to live in a thkythcraper!"

"A what?" said Aunt Janet, staring at her. It was not always easy to translate what Maisie was saying.

"A *skyscraper!*" gasped Macpherson.

He had often looked up at the high houses and wondered what it would be like to live so near the sky. He had watched them being built, one floor above the other, till they almost vanished from sight. No wonder they were called *sky*scrapers! As for living in one, he had never dreamt that *that* might happen.

Aunt Janet was still staring at Maisie as if she was the cause of all the trouble. "Nonsense!" she snapped. "They'll never get *me* up there!"

"Oh yes, they will!" Grandpa gave a chuckle. "They'll haul you up in one of the big cranes. *Ho-ro! Up she rises!*"

Grandpa seemed to be taking everything in his stride. His gaiety was so infectious that they all burst out laughing, even the budgie. Aunt Janet filled up the teapot, and they began the meal all over again, with a better appetite this time.

Maisie's face was soon smeared with strawberry jam. Even Aunt Janet did justice to the pancakes, though she stopped now and again to declare, "I won't go!" to which Grandpa always replied, "Oh yes, you will!"

"I'm full!" said Maisie, having eaten the last crumb of gingerbread. "Can I go and thpeak to the budgie?"

"No, you can just go," said Aunt Janet.

Maisie knew by the tone of her voice that there was no use protesting. "Oh well," she said, "I'll go and thpeak to the twinth." She trailed to the door in her one slipper. "I'll maybe thee you later, Macpherthon?"

"Maybe yes, and maybe no," said Macpherson, not giving himself away. "Cheerio, Maisie."

While Aunt Janet washed the dishes, Grandpa and Macpherson sat together at the window, as they always did. Macpherson looked up at the old man and said, "What do you really think of it, Grandpa? How will you like living in a skyscraper?"

A sad look came into Grandpa's eyes, and

Macpherson realised that much of his gaiety had been put on. He had as little wish as Aunt Janet to leave the shabby old tenement and make a new home, at his time of life. But he was used to facing difficulties and making the best of things. So he shrugged his shoulders and smiled at Macpherson. "It'll be an adventure, my boy. We'll weather the storm! Come on, now, Macpherson! Tell me every single thing that happened today, and no more secrets."

"No more secrets," promised Macpherson.

This was what he liked best, sharing everything with Grandpa. They talked on together, while Joey swung to and fro in his cage as if he had lived there for ever.

"Ship ahoy!" cried Grandpa, poking his finger through the bars and letting the bird peck at it. "Look at him, listening to every word we say! Oh well, he's one of the family now. All the same, Macpherson, we'd better find out if somebody's looking for him. Better put a notice in Murphy's shop-window. But I hope nobody claims him. He's a fine shipmate!"

Macpherson found a piece of paper and wrote out the notice:

BUDGIE FOUND WITH BLUE STRIPES.

ANSWERS TO NAME OF JOEY.

APPLY NUMBER FIVE, CLYDE-VIEW TENEMENTS.

As he wrote it out he wondered what his next address would be. "When—when is it going to happen, Grandpa?" he asked, hoping Grandpa would say, "Never! It's all a mistake, Macpherson, my boy. We can stay on here for ever and ever."

Grandpa shook his head, looking suddenly old and weary. "Soon, I believe. You ask Murphy. He knows everything."

Murphy's shop was very different from Mr McGlashan's—more like an Old Curiosity Shop, with a little bit of everything in it, even a white kitten sunning herself in the window.

Murphy was a stout, cheerful man who took each day as it came, let his customers run up bills, and always had time to stand at the door and chat.

"Hullo, Macpherson, my boyo! What's the hurry?"

"Would you put this in the window, please, Mr Murphy, and when are we going to be pulled down?" Macpherson said it all in the one breath.

Murphy studied the notice first. "A budgie, is it? Sure, I'll put it in the window, but it'll not be there long. The window, I mean. They're starting next week, and bad luck to them!" Murphy did his best to look angry, but only succeeded in looking comical. His face was not used to frowning.

"Next week!" gasped Macpherson. "That doesn't give us much time. Where—where are we going to, Mr Murphy?"

"Up to the sky, me boyo! See! that new one over there? Clyde-View Tower, they call it. Begob! I never thought Mick Murphy would be as near heaven."

He gave way to a fit of laughter while Macpherson gazed at the distant skyscraper. His new home! Imagine living away up there! What would it be like? How would he and Grandpa and Aunt Janet fit into a split-new place like that? It looked so bare and unhomely, fit for robots, maybe, but not for human beings.

Macpherson came back to earth with a feeling of guilt. He was always thinking of himself. What about Murphy? A new supermarket was being built beside the skyscraper, very different from the Old Curiosity Shop. How would Murphy make a living?

"Bedad! and that's the problem!" said Murphy, as though he had read Macpherson's thoughts. "There's not much hope for the small shop nowadays. But I've got me plans made and me fingers crossed." He leaned towards the boy and confided in him. "I've got me eye on an old van."

"A travelling shop!" cried Macpherson.

"That's right, me boyo! I'll go round all me old customers. Never say die! Sure, it'll be fun!"

Macpherson left him with a lighter heart. Murphy was right. There was always fun and adventure in life if one faced up to it in the right way.

3

Macpherson Goes Sky-High

"Message-boys! They'd drive you dotty! Macpherson! Stop standing about like a knotless thread! Get into the back-shop and look slippy!"

"Okay, Mr McGlashan, sir! I'll look slippy!"

Macpherson hurried into the back-shop, looking as slippy as he could. It was still in an untidy mess; but at least the policemen had gone. So now he and Miss Peacock could get down to the task of clearing up.

Macpherson grabbed a brush and set to. "Have they found anyone yet?" he asked Miss Peacock, who was down on her knees picking up some broken glass.

"They've got their eye on some suspects," she told him. "A gang called the Tarzans, I believe."

"Them!" cried Macpherson in surprise. "They're just boys! Well, youths, anyway!" He had seen signs of them often enough—BEWARE OF THE TARZANS—chalked up on walls and in bus-shelters. He had seen the gang, too, roaming the streets. There was nothing Tarzan-like about them. They seemed an aimless crowd of in-betweens, with too much time on their hands.

"Whoever they are, they've done plenty of damage," sighed Miss Peacock. "How are things with you, Macpherson?"

"Oh, Miss Peacock, you'll never guess! We're going to live in a skyscraper!"

"Goodness gracious me!" Miss Peacock sat back on her heels and looked up at him. "Tell me all about it, Macpherson."

That was one of the nice things about Miss Peacock. She was interested. It would be no use telling Old Skinflint; he would not care. But Miss Peacock was different. Like Grandpa, she always wanted to hear every single detail; and today Macpherson had plenty of details to tell her.

He took a deep breath and told her everything—about the budgie, the buildings coming down, about Murphy's shop and about the skyscraper. All the time he was careful to keep on working, knowing only too well that the grocer had his eye on him.

Mr McGlashan was behind the counter, but he kept the door into the back-shop open, and called through at intervals: "Don't dawdle!" "Time means money!" "Less talking and more work!" "Get on with it!"

Macpherson got on with his work and his story at the same time. He had made good headway with both when the grocer called through to him: "Macpherson! bring your basket! I've got some groceries for you to deliver."

When Macpherson saw the pile of groceries on the counter he said, "Mercy me!" and went back to fetch his biggest basket. He hoped he was not in for a long trail with *that* lot!

"They're for a new customer," said Old Skinflint, packing the basket full to the brim. "I've put the eggs on top. For goodness' sake, don't shoogle them, or I'll flay you alive!"

"Okay, Mr McGlashan, sir. I won't shoogle them," promised Macpherson, lifting the basket from the counter. It took two hands and all his strength to do the job. "What's the address?"

"Here!" The grocer thrust a piece of paper at him. "I've written it down in case you forget it. I know *your* woolly brain!"

Macpherson took a look at the address. BRUCE, 17 B, CALEDONIA COURT. It sounded very grand.

"Where's that?" he asked Old Skinflint.

"Message-boys! Do you not know your Glasgow? It's that new block up the road."

"What?" gasped Macpherson. "You mean the high houses?"

"Of course I mean the high houses. It's a skyscraper. Mrs Bruce lives on the seventeenth floor. Seventeen B. It's written down there on the paper. What more would your Lordship like to know?" asked the grocer in a sarcastic voice.

Macpherson would have liked to know many things, but he only risked asking one question: "How—how do I get up there?"

The grocer clicked his tongue impatiently. "You can fly up for all I care! Stop asking silly questions and get a move on. Message-boys! They put years on me!"

Macpherson lugged the heavy basket up the street, gazing ahead at the high houses. He had seen them often enough before, set in a group of five, as if they were giants ready to do a dance. They were much the same as the ones being built at Clyde-View. What fun it would be to see inside them, and tell Grandpa all about it when he got home!

The five giants all had different names: Lomond Court, Scotia Court, Argyll Court, Renfrew Court and Caledonia Court. Macpherson had to hunt till he found the one he wanted.

His message-basket was growing heavier every minute, so heavy that he could only go a few steps before laying it down. The giants, towering over him, made him feel very small, weak and puny.

He craned his neck and tried to count his way up to the seventeenth floor. "Eleven—twelve—

thirteen—goodness! it's nearly up to the sky!" he gasped.

"What's your trouble, young fellow?" A man in uniform spoke to him. He was not a policeman, nor a postman. "I'm the caretaker," he explained, jingling a bunch of keys. "Are you going up?"

"Yes," said Macpherson, still not sure how he was going to manage it.

"Come on, then! Through this way! Is it odd or even?"

Macpherson looked puzzled. "Odd or even?"

"The number! Is it an odd number or an even number?"

"Oh!" said Macpherson, understanding. "It's odd! Seventeen B!"

"Right! Press that button!"

There were two lifts—one for the odd numbers and one for the even numbers. Macpherson pressed the right button and waited for the lift to come down. It was away up on one of the high floors.

"Okay?" asked the man.

"Okay!" said Macpherson. "Thanks!"

While Macpherson waited for the lift, the caretaker got busy with a mop and brush. He was trying to clean some chalk marks off the wall. Macpherson caught a glimpse of the words before they were washed away—BEWARE OF THE TARZANS.

His heart gave a leap. "Mercy me!" he gasped. "Have that lot been here?"

"They're everywhere!" said the man as he rubbed the wall angrily with his mop. "Silly young things! What they need is a good.... Look out! Here's the lift!"

Macpherson hauled his basket inside. Then he stood on tiptoe to press the right button. Seventeen! The doors shut and he was a prisoner, sailing upwards to the sky. What would happen if the lift didn't stop? Or if it stuck? He would be a prisoner all right!

"Grandpa'll like this!" he thought. No trudging upstairs on his shaky legs. "Wait till I tell him!"

The lift stopped and doors opened as if by magic. Macpherson lifted his basket and hurried out before they could close again. Careful! Not an egg must be shoogled!

Where was he? In a strange, silent otherworld? There was no one about. Not a sound except the muffled music of a pop song from behind a closed door. Nothing but concrete walls and swing doors leading to empty passages—and a *view!*

Macpherson forgot everything else when he saw the view. He dumped down his basket, eggs and all, and ran to the side to look out over the city. Glasgow! "Jings!" he gasped, seeing his own city for the first time all-of-a-piece. "What a great big place!"

There it lay beneath him like an outsize map come to life. What a fine way to learn geography! He ran from side to side trying to locate all the landmarks. He could see the Clyde, of course, winding its way past the shipyards. He could see the canal, the churches, the streets, the parks—

and away in the distance, the hills! That was what amazed Macpherson most.

"Fancy seeing *hills* from the middle of the town!"

Macpherson could have stood and stared for ever. He tried to pinpoint the places he knew best—McGlashan's shop, for example. Yes! there it was, with toy cars passing the door and little people, as small as dwarfs, walking on the pavement. Was that his friend, the Highland bobby, at the corner? Yes, it was! The smallest policeman in the world!

He took a long time to find his own home. There were so many other things to see on the way. The parks seemed like small gardens. In one of them he could see men in striped jerseys playing football. They looked like little wasps running about the field.

The ships on the river seemed even smaller than the ones Grandpa made. He followed its course through the city, trying to find Clyde-View Tenements. There it was! next to the new skyscraper where *he* was going to live. He waved, though he knew he was too far off for Grandpa to see him.

"Yoo-hoo, Grandpa! Look at me! Away up near the sky!"

He looked up. There were still several floors

above him. What must it be like on the roof? There would be an even better bird's-eye view of the city. Up there, if he put out a hand, he could almost touch the clouds.

Macpherson came down to earth when he heard the lift-doors open. He turned round and hurried to pick up his basket. Too late! Two youths, coming out of the lift, pushed him aside. The bigger of the two, took hold of the basket and cried, "Hi, you! What are you doing up here? And what's in that basket? Stolen goods? *We'd* better take it from you."

"No, no!" cried Macpherson. "You'll shoogle the eggs!"

He tried to grab the basket, but his tormentors were too strong for him. They pushed and shoved and tugged it out of his grasp. Then one of them put out a sly foot and tripped him up. Down he fell on the concrete floor and lay sprawling there.

A frightening thought came into Macpherson's mind. Perhaps they were members of that gang—the Tarzans! If so, there was no hope for him. They were laughing at him now, as they rummaged about in the basket, to see what they could find. *Smash!* went the eggs! "Oh goodness gracious!" said Macpherson helplessly. What on earth would Old Skinflint say?

"What's going on?"

A door opened—the door of Number Seventeen B. Macpherson caught sight of a big fierce-looking woman, fierce enough to frighten off the youths. With a final kick at the basket, they fled through the swing-doors. And that was the end of them, apart from the sound of their footsteps as they ran down the stone stairs.

"That lot again! They're a menace!" said the woman as she grabbed the basket. "What a mess!" she said, looking at the contents. "Are you from McGlashan's?"

"Yes," said Macpherson, picking himself up.

"I'm sorry about the eggs. I don't know what Old Skin . . . . I mean, Mr McGlashan'll say. He'll kill me!"

"Not him! I'll explain!" she hauled both Macpherson and the basket through the doorway of Number Seventeen B. "Come in, and I'll ring him up. What's your name?"

"Macpherson!"

"What? Same here! Shake hands!"

Her idea of shaking hands made Macpherson wince with pain. Her grip was stronger than a man's.

"I thought your name was Bruce," he said, as she pushed him through the narrow hallway into the sitting-room.

"So it is, though most people just call me Mrs B. I was a Macpherson before I married *him*."

She pointed to a picture on the mantelpiece of a mild-looking man in policeman's uniform. "Dead!" she went on. "But I've taken his place."

"In the police force?" asked Macpherson, not that it surprised him. She looked tough enough to be in the Flying Squad.

She nodded. "Policewoman! Off-duty at the moment. Would you like a cup of tea?"

"Well . . . ."

"If it's Mr McGlashan you're worrying about, let's ring him up and be done with it."

She grabbed the telephone—Mrs B seemed to grab everything rather than lift it—while Macpherson took a look round the room. Everything was plain and scrubbed, with no nonsense about it, like Mrs B herself. There were no fancy cushions on the chairs. No frilly curtains at the window. But who needed frills with such a view?

Macpherson hurried across to look out. There it was again! How wonderful it must be to see the city and the sky and the hills like this every day, without even going outside! Grandpa had a treat in store for him.

Mrs B was talking to Old Skinflint. Telling him off! Macpherson wished *he* had the nerve to talk to the grocer like that!

"Nonsense!" she was saying. "The boy couldn't help it. Listen to me! He was set upon by a gang. Yes, a *gang!*" She winked across at Macpherson. "No, no. The groceries are all right. It's the message-boy who's shaken." She winked again at Macpherson. "I'm keeping him here for a while, till he recovers."

Macpherson could hear Old Skinflint speaking in the voice he used for his customers. "Yes, Mrs Bruce! Of course, Mrs Bruce! As long as *you* have no complaints."

"None at all! Not about Macpherson! He

seems a fine boy! You're lucky to have him!" Another wink.

Macpherson was surprised to hear Old Skinflint agreeing with her. "Oh yes, I know, Mrs Bruce. A fine boy! I'm very lucky! You'll be sending in another order soon?"

"Of course; and you'll send Macpherson to deliver it. Goodbye, Mr McGlashan!" She slammed down the receiver. "That's settled him! Now we can enjoy our tea."

The tea was so strong that Macpherson could scarcely swallow it. All the same, Mrs B was a kind hostess, in spite of her rough ways. She brought out a tin of biscuits—plain like herself—and said, "Eat up! You're far too thin. Tell me about yourself."

Between bites of biscuit and gulps of strong tea, Macpherson told her. Mrs B gave a grunt now and then as she listened. "Clyde-View Tenements! High time *they* came down! You'll be better off in the new skyscraper. I'll keep my eye on you. I'm often round that way. As for that grocer fellow, why not stand up to him?"

Why not, indeed? It was all very well for Mrs B. *She* was a customer as well as a policewoman.

"I'll try," he promised. "Thanks for the tea, Mrs B. You've been very kind."

"Rubbish!"

Macpherson was glad she did not try to shake hands again. Yet, as he went down in the lift, he felt a warm glow at his heart, as if he had made a real friend. He could face up to anything—even Old Skinflint—if Mrs B was behind him.

Outside, he craned his neck to look up. Yes! there she was at the window—as small as a pigmy now—giving him a salute. Macpherson saluted back, and went on his way, whistling.

If he had expected Old Skinflint to receive him with open arms, he was very much mistaken. The grocer was grumpier than ever. It was one thing being polite to customers. There was no need to be polite to message-boys. Keep them in their place!

"So! You've decided to come back at last! Very kind of you, I'm sure!" Old Skinflint gave him an angry glare. "How often have I told you to keep out of the way of these gangs? But what's the use of talking to message-boys! They've got no sense! Get into the back-shop and do some work!"

For a moment Macpherson thought of answering him back—but only for a moment. One look at Old Skinflint's sour face made him change his mind. If only Mrs B had been there!

"Okay, Mr McGlashan, sir," said Macpherson meekly. "I'm going!"

Miss Peacock was still down on her knees, with a newspaper spread out in front of her. She pointed to the LOST AND FOUND column. "Look, Macpherson!" she cried. "What d'you think of this?"

He squatted down beside her and read the notice. *Lost, budgie with blue stripes, answering to name of Joey. Finder please return to 15 Carlton Mansions. Good reward.*

"Oh dear!" Macpherson's face fell. "What'll I do?"

"You'd better take the budgie back, Macpherson," said Miss Peacock gently. She had a great sense of right and wrong. "Think of the owner."

Macpherson could only think of Grandpa, sitting at the window with Joey swinging in his cage near by. The old man had already begun to teach the bird some new words. Macpherson had left the two of them this morning whistling happily to each other. How could he go home and break the bad news to Grandpa that he was to lose his new pet?

"Your Grandpa wouldn't want to keep Joey, knowing he belonged to someone else," said Miss Peacock sensibly. "You know the right thing to do, Macpherson."

"Yes," he said with a sigh. He took a closer

look at the newspaper. "Carlton Mansions! Where's that, Miss Peacock?"

"It's one of those luxury flats in the West End. They cost a fortune, I'm told. The people living there must be millionaires. You'll get a good reward," Miss Peacock told him.

"I'd sooner keep the budgie," said Macpherson sadly. "Oh dear! Poor Grandpa!"

For the rest of the day he could think of nothing else. Old Skinflint kept him busy, but his mind was not on his work. He scrubbed shelves; he swept floors; he ran here and there with baskets of groceries. But all the time he was thinking of Grandpa trying to teach Joey to say, "Heave-ho, my hearty!"

At last it was locking-up time. The grocer's parting words to Macpherson were, "I hope you'll look a bit sharper tomorrow. Message-boys! They've got nothing in their heads but cotton-wool."

At the door Miss Peacock pulled on her gloves and smiled at him. "Straight home, Macpherson?"

"No," said he, suddenly making up his mind. "I'm away to Carlton Mansions."

The luxury flats were very different from the skyscrapers. Not so high, for one thing; far grander, for another. They were set back from the road in a well-kept garden. Every flower stood up straight, looking like a prize specimen. Not a weed in sight!

Macpherson felt shabby and threadbare as he walked down the pathway. At the entrance he hesitated. A man dressed in a uniform grander than an admiral's was guarding the door. He looked down at Macpherson from a great height.

"Oh no! not another!" he groaned, pushing back his gold-braided hat. "Where's yours, then? In your pocket?"

"What?" said Macpherson, puzzled. Then suddenly he caught sight of a crowd inside the hallway—men, women and children—all with something in common. Each was carrying a bird-cage with a budgie inside.

4

His Nibs

"They're all after the reward," said the porter, with a look of disgust. "Budgies! I never saw so many in my life."

"But they can't all be the right one!" said Macpherson, amazed. "Surely they can't *all* answer to the name of Joey!"

"You'd be surprised, young man! There are hundreds of budgies in Glasgow called Joey. I've seen at least two dozen today already. They're queueing up!"

"Mercy me!" Macpherson began to see a ray of hope. If there were as many as all that, there was every chance that his budgie was safe.

"Where is it, then?" the man was asking him. "Up your sleeve?"

"No, it's at home."

The man pushed his hat right to the back of his head. "What? D'you mean to say *you*'re not after the reward?"

"No, I'm not! I'd sooner keep Joey," said Macpherson. And he told the man the whole story.

The porter heard him out and then said, "I believe every word of it, which is more than I do with some of the tales I've heard today! You'd better go up and tell it to His Nibs."

"Who's he?" asked Macpherson.

"He's the one who's lost the budgie. Second floor! Take the lift! Best of luck!"

Macpherson had to wait his turn for the lift. There were so many goings-up with budgies in all kinds of cages, and so many comings-down with the budgies still in the cages.

"Oh dear, he still hasn't found the right one," thought Macpherson, looking worried. His hopes were beginning to fade. "Poor Grandpa!"

At last it was his turn. The lift was much grander than the one in the skyscraper. Everything was shining and polished. There was a seat inside, covered with a velvet cushion. There was a mirror and a vase of real flowers. There was even a carpet on the floor, with two or three budgerigar feathers lying on it.

Macpherson pushed the right button. The lift sailed up smoothly and silently. The doors opened gently and he found himself in a polished hallway. First on the right! He peered at the name-plate. Who was His Nibs, he wondered?

There were two names, with a hyphen between them: BIGGS-BROWN. Macpherson braced himself and rang the bell. He could hear its musical chime—*ding-dong-ding*—as if it were playing a tune.

A Chinese servant in a white coat opened the door. "Come in, please," he said in a sing-song voice. He led Macpherson towards another door and said, "Please sir, here's one more, sir."

Macpherson stood in the doorway looking for His Nibs. All he could see was a boy sitting on the floor playing with a train-set.

Such a train-set! It was an entire railway-system. Signals! Tunnels! Stations! Engines! Goods-trains! There was even one called *The Flying Scotsman!* The boy had only to press a button and they went racing round the track, in and out of tunnels, stopping at stations, shunting into sidings. Macpherson stood and stared. Fancy having a toy like that! It must have cost a fortune.

The boy was younger than Macpherson, with a darker skin, as if he had been used to a hot climate. But there was nothing sunny about his expression. He was frowning at the trains as he made them go faster, and there was a fretful note in his voice as he spoke. "Well, where is it?" he asked, without looking up.

"Where's what?" Macpherson was not going to be spoken to like that by any young boy, no

matter how many trains he had!

"My budgie, of course!"

"Oh!" said Macpherson, staring at him. "Are *you* His Nibs?"

The boy stopped the trains, sat back on his heels and looked up at him. "My name's Barnaby Biggs-Brown," he said in a haughty voice. "You can call me sir."

"Away!" scoffed Macpherson, half-amused, half-angry. "I'll punch your nose!"

"What?" His Nibs grew red in the face and sprang to his feet clenching his small fists. "You watch it, or I'll have you thrown out!"

"You needn't bother," said Macpherson coolly. "I'm going!"

"Wait!" The boy called him back as if he were speaking to a slave. "What about my budgie?"

"Your budgie? What about it?" Macpherson scowled at His Nibs who glared back at him. "I've certainly found one, but I don't know if it's yours."

"Tell me what it says, and I'll soon know. Come along! Be quick about it!"

"I'll take my time!" said Macpherson sharply. The impudence of him! Everything His Nibs said rubbed him up the wrong way. "Let me think! What does the budgie say? Oh yes! 'How d'you do? Joey's a bonnie wee boy ....' "

"Rubbish!" said His Nibs, with his nose in the air. "*My* budgie would never say anything so silly!"

"Good! That's a relief!" burst out Macpherson. "I can keep mine! Okay, then! I'm off!"

"Stop!" Once more the boy called him back. "You haven't told me who you are or where you live."

Macpherson could not help smiling at the

small boy standing in front of him, like a little cock-sparrow, full of his own importance. No use getting angry with him. His Nibs was only a spoilt child in need of a spanking.

"It's none of your business," said Macpherson in a teasing voice. "But if you must know, my name's Macpherson and I live at Clyde-View Tenements."

"In the slums?" The boy gave him a pitying glance and drew himself up to his full height. "*My* name's Barnaby Biggs-Brown and I live here, when we're not abroad. My father's away just now. *He*'s a general."

"Good for him!" said Macpherson. "Well, the best of luck to you! Cheerio, Your Nibs. I'm away home to Grandpa."

"Hold on!" The boy seemed anxious to detain him. "Wouldn't you like to see my toys? I've got a whole room full of them."

"No, thanks," said Macpherson, making for the door. "You play with your train."

The boy gave the train a kick. "I'm sick of that old thing," he said in a peevish voice. "I wish I had my budgie back."

The doorbell played its musical chime. "Perhaps this is it," said Macpherson cheerfully. "I'm away this time. Cheerio!"

"Will you come back and see me again?"

There was a pleading note in the boy's voice.

"Maybe yes and maybe no." Macpherson was not going to commit himself. One visit to His Nibs was enough!

"Oh well," said the boy, giving him up. "Ching will show you out." He called to the servant. "Ching! The door!"

"Yes, master! I go!"

As Macpherson was shown out, another visitor was shown in—a stout man clutching a bird-cage. Macpherson hoped, for the boy's sake, that it was the right one this time. He did not wait for the lift but ran down the stairs, whistling. Maybe it was not so bad, after all, being poor. He had no room full of toys, but at least he had Grandpa, and was far too busy to feel lonely or bored.

Maisie Murphy was sitting on her doorstep with a baby in her arms and a crowd of children around her. Some were Murphies, others came from nearby tenements. All were sucking their thumbs, for want of anything better, and staring at Maisie who was telling them a story.

"Tho Thinderella went to the ball! And d'you know what happened when the Printhe thaw her?"

No! Nobody had any idea, except the baby

who let out a loud: "Goo-oo-oo!" and blew a string of bubbles in Maisie's face.

"That'th right!" she said, shoogling the baby up and down. "The Printhe took one look at Thinderella and thaid....Oh! here'th Macpherthon!"

Who was Prince Charming compared with her own hero? She gave up the story and stood up. "Mac-pher-thon!" she called out, as he tried to hurry past. "D'you know what?"

"No, I don't! Away you go, Maisie Murphy! I'm not wanting any of your fairy-stories."

"But thith ith a *real* thtory," she insisted.

"Okay then," said Macpherson, pausing for a moment. "It had better be good!"

Maisie's story was not so much good as startling!

"Your Grandpa'th not at home!"

"What?" Macpherson stared at her. "Where is he?"

"He'th away!"

"Where?" asked Macpherson in alarm.

Maisie shook her head. "He'th lotht! Your Auntie'th been out looking for him...."

Macpherson did not wait to hear more. He went racing away to Number Five and rushed up the stairs two at a time. His heart was thumping when he reached the top. Grandpa lost! It was the worst thing in the world that could have happened.

Aunt Janet was pacing up and down the kitchen, stopping now and again to take a quick look out of the window.

"Where is he? What's happened? Where can he have gone? Do *you* know anything about it?" She rounded on Macpherson, prepared to be angry with him, but he shook his head. She could be as cross as she liked. *He* knew the reason. "No, I've no idea, Aunt Janet. I've only just heard from Maisie. How long has he been away?"

"I don't know. I came in about an hour ago, and the place was empty. I've been here, there and everywhere, looking for him. Murphy's shop! The public library! The park. . . ."

"But Grandpa would never go there on his own," burst out Macpherson, white with fear. The old man's legs were too shaky to get up and down stairs without someone helping him. As for crossing the street. . . . what if he had been knocked down and was lying hurt in hospital? Or dead? Macpherson's face went even whiter.

"He's gone somewhere on his own! Wait till I get hold of him!" said Aunt Janet, pretending to be her usual cross self. But Macpherson knew, by her trembling voice, that she was feeling every bit as miserable as he was. How could he comfort her?

"It—it'll be all right, Aunt Janet. I'll go out and look for him. Maybe the Highland bobby'll help me."

But first he went to the window to have a final look out. Usually it was the other way round—Grandpa looking for him. The sight of the old man waving and smiling always spurred the boy on, no matter how weary he was. How terrible if he never saw Grandpa again at the window!

Suddenly he made a discovery. The budgie was gone! The cage had been taken down from its hook above the window. What was worse, a newspaper lay open on the table. Grandpa's spectacles were there, lying on the LOST AND FOUND column. *Lost, budgie with blue stripes, answering to name of Joey.*

"I know!" Macpherson cried out. "The budgie!"

"What?" Aunt Janet had been too worried to notice that the budgerigar had gone. "What do you mean? Has he taken it away?"

Macpherson nodded and began to explain. He could see it all! The old man peering at the newspaper and suddenly realising that Joey belonged to someone else. Knowing Grandpa, Macpherson was sure that the old man could not bear the thought of keeping someone else's property. He must have taken Joey to Carlton Mansions! But how had they missed each other? Had Grandpa lost his way, or been run over?

"Carlton Mansions!" cried Aunt Janet. "But that's miles away. Think of all the streets he'd have to cross!" She turned on Macpherson. "You and your Grandpa! If it's not one it's the other! You've not got a drop of sense between you!"

"Look, Aunt Janet! There he is!"

Macpherson was staring down into the street at a long sleek car weaving its way past Maisie

and her gang of children. At the wheel sat Ching, the Chinese servant, and in the back—Grandpa and His Nibs. The old man seemed to be in the highest spirits, waving cheerfully to Maisie as Ching leapt out to open the door.

"A Chinaman!" cried Aunt Janet. "What next?"

The next to come out was His Nibs holding the bird-cage. "That's him! The boy I was telling you about," Macpherson explained to Aunt Janet. "Barnaby Biggs-Brown! They call him His Nibs. I hope *he's* not coming up."

But he was! Macpherson felt a twinge of jealousy when he saw the boy take Grandpa by the hand to steady him. He wanted to call down, "Leave him alone! He's *my* Grandpa!" But just then Grandpa looked up. He grinned and waved, and pointed upwards as much as to say, "We'll soon be up! Put the kettle on!"

Aunt Janet stamped around the kitchen in a fury of activity, tidying up. "The idea!" she raged, "bringing a young lord up here, and the place like a pig-sty!"

"He'll never notice. He's only a boy," said Macpherson sulkily, and went to the door. He could hear Grandpa and His Nibs laughing and talking as they came nearer. They seemed to be the best of friends already.

Macpherson shuffled his feet and felt his anger rising. He wanted to run down to meet Grandpa, but not with that boy there. What right had His Nibs to take his place?

"Ahoy there, Macpherson!"

"Ahoy, Grandpa!" In spite of himself, Macpherson could not keep the happiness out of his voice. It was so wonderful to have Grandpa home, safe and sound. Forgetting his jealousy, he ran down to help him up the last few steps. "Oh, Grandpa! I'm awful glad to see you!"

"Same here, Macpherson, my boy! Glad to be home!" The old man was puffing and panting by now. "Easy does it! One more step and I'm there! Upsi-daisy!"

With a helping hand on each side he reached the door and made straight for his shabby old armchair. He eased himself down and looked up at Aunt Janet. "Well, Janet woman, I'm back! What about a cup of tea?"

That was enough for Aunt Janet! Never mind the "young lord" standing at the door, listening. She had bottled it up long enough. Now she let fly with her tongue.

"A cup of tea! I'll give you more than a cup of tea! Where have you been? You're worse than Macpherson, and that's saying a lot! Going off like that, with never a word, at your time of life!

You might have been run over, and serve you right...."

Grandpa put his hands to his ears to stem the flow. "Stop, woman, stop! I'm old enough to take care of myself." He grinned up at her like a naughty child. "Forget it, Janet woman, and put on the kettle. See! we've got a visitor. Come in, young Barnaby."

The boy came in, carrying the bird-cage. Macpherson took it from him and hung it back on the hook by the window. "Thank goodness, we can still keep Joey," said Grandpa, turning to Macpherson. "Wait till you hear all my adventures! I hear you've met Barnaby?"

"Yes," said Macpherson briefly. He gave His Nibs a look which was far from friendly. Why didn't the boy go away and leave them in peace? What *he* wanted was to hear Grandpa's story, and to tell him all about his own adventures in the skyscraper. But not with a stranger listening.

His Nibs was gazing round the kitchen. No doubt he had never seen such a bare, shabby place before. Suddenly he sat down on a stool at Grandpa's feet—Macpherson's place—and looked up at the old man. "You said you'd show me your ships-in-bottles," he said eagerly. "Where are they?"

The old man pointed to the mantelpiece, and said, with a note of pride in his voice, "There's one up there: the *Hebridean*. A fine ship! I used to sail in her myself. I'm making another one, over there by the window: the *Indian Queen*. I'll show it to you after we've had our tea."

Macpherson stood in the background feeling left out. Grandpa and His Nibs seemed to have so much in common. The old man had been round the world in his sailing days. So had young Barnaby Biggs-Brown. At least, he had visited many foreign countries with his father. India! Japan! Africa! Young though he was, he seemed to have seen and done everything.

The boy looked happier now. There was less of the young lord about him, now that he had found someone to take an interest in him. He chatted happily to Grandpa while Macpherson's face grew more and more sulky. What right had that boy to sit at Grandpa's feet, taking up the old man's attention?

"It's only a plain tea," said Aunt Janet, dumping a plateful of scones on the table. "Come and get it, if you want it."

Grandpa and His Nibs went and sat at the table, but for once Macpherson had lost his appetite.

"I'll go down and get some coals," he mumbled, and grabbed the pail. It was his favourite retreat—the coal-cellar in the back-court—when he was out of sorts. He could hide therc in peace, with no one to disturb him.

The Chinese servant gave him a salute as he reached the door. Maisie called out, "Mac-pherthon!" in a hopeful voice, but he took no notice of either of them. In the dark coal-cellar, with the door shut, he sat down on an upturned pail and thought his own thoughts.

It was a long hard fight; but he won the battle

in the end. Gradually he began to calm down. Why was he worrying about such a trifle? How much worse it would have been if Grandpa had never come back! Surely it was better to share him, once in a while, than not to have him at all.

"He'th away!"

Maisie was rattling at the door. Macpherson had no idea how much time had passed. All he knew was that a load had lifted from his heart. Everything was all right again.

He whistled as he filled the coal-pail. His steps on the stairs were light. When he entered the kitchen he smiled at Grandpa in his old way.

"Ahoy there, Macpherson!" Grandpa knew and understood. "Young Barnaby's away! Poor laddie! he's not as lucky as we are. He's got everything except folk to care for him. Come away! Sit down and tell me every single thing."

5

All Aboard the Skyscraper

"All aboard! Hullo, Macpherson, my boy! Ship ahoy!"

It was not Grandpa who was speaking. It was Joey the budgie, who was rapidly learning to imitate everyone in the household. He could say, "Hullo, Grandpa!" in Macpherson's voice. He could copy Aunt Janet when she was scolding. He could even lisp like Maisie: "Mac-pher-thon!" He was, in fact, one of the family.

Grandpa spent long happy hours teaching him to talk. "Did you hear that, Macpherson?" he said proudly. "He's coming on! Joey's a clever wee boy!"

"A clever wee boy!" agreed the budgie, swinging to and fro in his cage.

The cage was the only thing still left in its proper place in the kitchen. Everything else was in the middle of the floor, waiting to be packed up. Today was their last day in Number Five, Clyde-View Tenements.

"Keep that bird quiet!" snapped Aunt Janet

in an irritated voice. "Macpherson, what on earth's this?"

This was a box full of old toys—a broken soldier, a burst ball, a ship in a bottle, the remains of a kite Grandpa had once made. Unlike His Nibs, Macpherson had few treasures; but what he had, he liked to keep.

"They're mine!" he cried, guarding the box. "You're not to throw them out!"

Aunt Janet had been having a great clearance. Now that the time had come, she was too busy to feel sad or, at least, to show her feelings. Grandpa and Macpherson had to keep a close watch on her in case all their treasures were dumped in the dustbins.

"My old oilskins!" cried Grandpa, grabbing them from her. "You're not going to throw *them* out, Janet woman!"

"They're falling to bits!" protested Aunt Janet. "They're only fit for the rubbish-heap."

"Nothing of the sort!" Grandpa held them lovingly in front of him. "I wore them when I was rounding the Horn. Did I ever tell you about it, Macpherson?"

"Yes, Grandpa; but I'd like to hear it again," said Macpherson loyally.

"You'll do no such thing!" stormed Aunt Janet. "This is no time for story-telling. The removal-van will be here in no time, and us not half ready. Macpherson, have you been down to clear out the coal-cellar?"

"Yes, I have, Aunt Janet, but I'll go and have another look."

The truth was Macpherson wanted to say a last goodbye in private to his favourite hiding-place in the back-court. It had been a refuge to him so often in the past. What was he going to do without it in future? There would be no coal-cellars in the new skyscraper; not even a fireplace or a chimney. He was not sure there would be a back-green, or any place where he could seek shelter when he wanted to be alone.

It was all coming so near that he suddenly felt frightened. Grandpa knew what he was feeling. "Away you go, Macpherson," he said, patting him on the shoulder. "I'll keep an eye on *her* to see she doesn't throw everything out. If she had her way, she'd have me in the dustbin, too!"

"Don't talk nonsense!" said Aunt Janet sharply.

Her lips were tighter than ever today, but Macpherson knew why—she was trying to keep control of her feelings. Grandpa, for the same reason, was a little too cheerful. It was not easy for any of them to be normal on such a day.

Macpherson ran down the worn stairs and tried to dodge into the back-court without being seen, especially by Maisie. No such luck! At that very moment she came staggering out of her house, carrying the baby in one arm and a large pot plant in the other.

"Oh merthy me!" she said, dumping the plant on the pavement, "ithn't thith a day, Macpherthon?"

The Murphies were also getting ready to move out. Indeed, some of their shabby furniture was already in the street. A grandfather clock leaned against an old chair with uneven legs. A wardrobe with the door swinging open revealed a collection of odd clothes. Frying-pans, mirrors, china dogs, jugs and cutlery were piled on a rickety table. The well-worn pram was full of cups, saucers, kettles and teapots.

Maisie, however, was used to chaos and took everything in her stride. She was even ready to lend a hand to her hero, if need be.

"Ith there anything I can do, Macpherthon?" she asked hopefully.

"Yes! Keep out of my way!" he said unkindly.

"All right," she said, not taking offence. "I'll go and bring out more thingth."

Macpherson went and sat for the last time in the empty coal-cellar, thinking his own thoughts. He went back over his life to the days when Grandpa had been able to play hide-and-seek with him, in Davy Jones' locker. Macpherson had always hidden in a dark corner, behind a heap of coals, where the old man pretended not to see him.

"No! He's not in here!" he would say. "Can't see him anywhere! Oh deary me! I'll never find him! The boy's lost!"

It was at this point that Macpherson always dashed out—to Grandpa's seeming surprise—

and ran to base, shouting in triumph: "I've won again, Grandpa!"

"So you have, my boy! You've got me beat!"

There were tears in Macpherson's eyes as he thought back to those old happy days. How often he and Grandpa had sat here, planning some small secret together, with no fear of interruption....

Bang! Bang! Bang!

Three loud knocks on the door! Macpherson leapt to his feet and cried, "Who's there?"

"It's me—Barnaby!"

For a moment Macpherson could not think who Barnaby was. Then suddenly it dawned on him. Barnaby Biggs-Brown! His Nibs!

Angrily he opened the door and glared at the small boy. "What are *you* doing here?" he asked in a cross voice.

"I came to tell you the vans have arrived," said His Nibs.

"So what? It's no business of yours!"

His Nibs tossed his head. "It is so! I've come to help. I've brought the car so that I can give your Grandpa a lift to the new place. You can come, too, if you like."

"No, thanks! I'll walk," said Macpherson, still in a huff.

At the back of his mind he knew he ought to be

grateful to His Nibs for thinking of helping Grandpa. All the same, this was a family affair. It would spoil everything, having a stranger poking his nose in.

"I'd like to punch it!" he said crossly, looking at Barnaby's small nose.

"What?" asked His Nibs, looking up at him.

"Oh, never mind," said Macpherson, pushing him aside.

"Is *this* where you used to play?" His Nibs was peering into the empty coal-cellar. "Your Grandpa said you used to have great times down here in Davy Jones' locker. It doesn't look much of a place to me."

Macpherson's temper rose. "Who cares what you think? I'll tell you what *I* think. . . ."

"You needn't bother!" broke in His Nibs. "Who are *you*, anyway? You're only a message-boy with a bad temper. I like your Grandpa better."

"He's *my* Grandpa, and don't you forget it! Buzz off and mind your own business!"

"I will not!" said the little cock-sparrow. "I'll fight you first!"

"Right! Put up your fists!"

They began sparring. It would have been easy enough for Macpherson to knock His Nibs down with one blow, but something stopped him. His

Nibs was so much smaller, for one thing. For another, he knew that Grandpa would not like it. The old man was sorry for young Barnaby. Why couldn't *he* feel the same, instead of getting angry with him?

It was Maisie who put an end to the fight.

"Thtop it!" she screamed, rushing in between them and narrowly missing getting her own nose punched. "You're a thilly boy!" she told His Nibs severely. (It was all *his* fault, of course!) "If you don't behave yourthelf, I'll-I'll thpank you!

Tho I will!"

She faced up to His Nibs, who stepped back, more frightened of her than of Macpherson. And no wonder! When Maisie was in a temper, her face grew bright scarlet, her eyes flashed with fire, and she looked so full of rage that she could easily have "thpanked" a giant. Added to this, she had put on all the odd clothes that had tumbled out of the wardrobe.

"You look a ticket!" jeered Macpherson, angry at having the fight stopped by the likes of her.

"I do not!" said Maisie. But she did!

There were two, if not three, hats perched on her head, one on top of the other. She was wearing Murphy's old overcoat, trailing to the ground, the pockets stuffed with well-worn baby clothes. Several scarves were wound round her neck, and in her hand she carried a tattered umbrella.

She held it in front of her like a spear and gave a final warning to Barnaby. "You go away and leave Macpherthon alone!"

Strangely enough, Macpherson now found himself standing up for His Nibs. "Dry up, Maisie!" he said sharply. "He's not doing any harm. It was only a game."

Maisie hitched up her trailing coat and said in

a grown-up voice, "Thith ith no time for playing. There'th work to be done. The vanth are waiting. Come on! Everythingth upthide-down!"

True enough, the Murphy furniture was in danger of getting mixed up with Aunt Janet's. The two vans stood side by side, with the Biggs-Brown car near by. The Chinese servant was no longer at the wheel. He was running up and down the tenement stairs, fetching and carrying with the removal men. Now and again he darted into the Murphy's house and came out with a baby or a bundle. His face was wreathed in smiles. Ching was enjoying all the stir and bustle.

"All hands to the helm!" cried Grandpa from the top of the stairs. He held the bird-cage in one hand and the *Hebridean* in the other. He was being extra cheerful to cover up his feelings.

"Wait there, Grandpa!" called Macpherson, racing up the stairs. "I'll come and help you down."

"Me, too!" cried His Nibs, trying to push past him.

In a moment of anger, Macpherson put out his foot to trip him up, then stopped himself in time. He had caught sight of Grandpa half-way down the stairs. The old man was shaking his head as much as to say, "Come now, Macpherson, my boy! No need to be jealous! Two boys are better than one!"

Indeed, the old man was so frail that it took the two of them all their time to get him down safely—but it was on Macpherson's arm that he leaned most heavily.

"Heave-ho, boys!" he said, as they helped him into the car. "I'll sit here like a lord and let you do all the work. Put Joey in beside me. He'll keep me company."

Grandpa leaned back on the cushions and took a last look at the crumbling tenement.

"Are you all right, Grandpa?" asked Macpherson anxiously. The old man's face seemed so white and strained.

"Yes, yes! Ship-shape, my boy!" said Grandpa, closing his eyes. "I'll just have forty winks till you're ready."

Macpherson was not sure if he was really having forty winks. How could anyone sleep with such a din going on? Was he closing his eyes to shut out the sight of his old home being taken to pieces? Macpherson tucked a rug round his knees, and went back to help the others.

Maisie had now found a willing slave. His Nibs, used to giving orders himself, was now meekly taking them from her. He seemed to like being bossed by Miss Murphy.

"Come on, you! Carry thith bathket into the van and don't drop it. It'th full of jugth. Then you can go and look for the twinth."

The twins were the trouble! Maisie was kept busy counting and recounting her flock, afraid that one would be left behind. The twins—Him and Her—had a habit of wandering away if no one kept an eye on them. His Nibs hunted high and low, even in the wardrobe, without success.

"I can't find them anywhere," he had to confess.

"Thilly thing! You're no good!" said Maisie, pushing him aside. "Here, hold the baby! I'll go and look mythelf." But even Maisie could not run them to earth.

Macpherson was about to join in the search when Aunt Janet rapped on the window and called down to him: "Macpherson! Come up here! I want you!"

For the last time he ran up the worn stairs. He had to wait on the landing to let the removal men past. One carried the kitchen table on his head. The other staggered under the weight of Grandpa's old armchair. Now there was nothing left—except Aunt Janet with her hat and coat on.

"What is it, Aunt Janet?" Macpherson looked round the desolate kitchen and tried to picture it as it had once been, cosy and homely.

There was a blotchy look on Aunt Janet's face, as if she had been crying again. "Get him away!" she said urgently. "It's bad for him, sitting there watching."

"Grandpa? But he's having a snooze. . . ."

"Not him! He just doesn't want to look. Can't you get the Chinaman to take him for a run in the car?"

"Oh yes, Aunt Janet! That's a good idea!"

"That young Nibs can go with him; but you'd better stay, Macpherson. I'll need you."

"Yes, Aunt Janet, I'll stay!" Imagine her needing him! She was still wandering about restlessly, taking a last look here and a last look there. On an impulse he grabbed her hand. "Come on, Aunt Janet! Downstairs! I'll shut the door! Quick! See who can get down first!"

"Don't be daft!" she cried. All the same, she came. Her face was flushed and her lips tight, but there were no more tears. She held her head high when she reached the street, and before long was having sharp words with the van-men.

Macpherson drew His Nibs aside. "Hi, you! will you do something for me?"

"Yes," said His Nibs, looking over his shoulder, "if Maisie lets me!"

"She's only a lassie! You do what I say," said

Macpherson, grabbing him by the arm. "Will you take Grandpa for a run, to keep him out of the way?"

"Oh yes, I will! A long run! We might go as far as Loch Lomond."

"What's that?" said Grandpa, with his eyes still shut. "*The bonnie bonnie banks....*"

"Joey's a bonnie wee boy!" chimed in the budgerigar, while His Nibs gave his orders to Ching and got in beside the old man.

"Wouldn't you like to come, too, Macpherson?" asked Grandpa, opening one eye.

"Yes, I would, but I can't!" Macpherson swallowed his jealousy and pretended not to care. "His Nibs'll look after you, and I'll hear all about it when you get back. Ch-cheerio, Grandpa! Enjoy yourself!"

Grandpa gave him a half-hearted wave—or was he waving goodbye to the tenement?—and the car glided away. It was no sooner out of sight than another car, small and sturdy, came tooting towards them. A big woman, in police uniform, sat very upright at the wheel. Bouncing about in the back were the Murphy twins.

"Mrs B!" cried Macpherson, opening the door for her. "What's brought *you* here?"

"I found these two wandering about," she explained. "It's not the first time I've brought them home! Do you need any help, Macpherson?"

Without waiting for an answer, Mrs B stepped out and took command. It was surprising how smoothly everything went under her control. The van-men put on a spurt. The Murphies rounded each other up. Even Aunt Janet allowed herself to be ordered about. And in next to no time they were all ready to move off.

"Goodbye, Clyde-View Tenements!" said Macpherson, with a lump in his throat, and turned his back on his old home.

"Oh, Aunt Janet! come and look at the view!"

"No, no! I can't stand it! It makes me dizzy! Besides, there's no time to stare out of the window. There's far too much to do. Get a move on, Macpherson! I want everything ship-shape before your Grandpa comes home."

Home! Clyde-View Tower, Number 22 A. It was strange to think of such a new place as "home". No one else had ever lived in it before. Indeed, the paint on the doors was hardly dry.

They were alone—Macpherson and Aunt Janet. The van-men had brought the shabby furniture up in the service lift and placed it where she wanted it. Now they were gone. Mrs B had also left, after dumping a hamper on the table.

"Your first meal," she said in her gruff voice. "I thought you might not have time to bother about food; but there's nothing like a good tuck-in when you're removing!"

A good tuck-in! There was a cooked chicken and some ham. There was an apple pie, and a chocolate cake. There was even a bottle of lemonade for Macpherson, a packet of tobacco for Grandpa and a bag of peppermints for Aunt Janet.

"Mrs B, you're a gem!" cried Macpherson. But Mrs B had rushed away, without waiting for a word of thanks.

Macpherson set the food on the kitchen table while Aunt Janet boiled the kettle. Everything must be ready for Grandpa when he came back. The boy tried to make it look as familiar as possible, with the old armchair in the same position, his stool beside it, and Grandpa's slippers and pipe at hand.

Every now and then Macpherson looked out of the window—down—down—down—into the street to see if the car was coming. Suddenly, there was a ring at the doorbell, a sharp, unfamiliar sound.

"If that's Maisie Murphy," began Aunt Janet—but it wasn't! It was a message-boy, not unlike Macpherson himself, with a large bouquet of flowers in his hand. There was a small note attached to it, in Miss Peacock's writing. *Happy landings in your new home.*

Aunt Janet got the sniffles when she read it and hurried through to her small bedroom. It was left to Macpherson to find a big enough vase and place the flowers on the centre of the table.

Another look out of the window! "Aunt Janet! he's here! He's getting out of the car! I'm away down to bring Grandpa up in the lift! Oh my! I wonder what he'll think of his new home?"

6

Meet the General

"For what we are about to receive," said Grandpa solemnly, bowing his head.

What they were about to receive was something extra-special—a birthday dumpling. There were plenty of other good things to eat on the table. A cake with pink icing stood in the centre. There were ham sandwiches and sausage rolls. There were chocolate biscuits and shortbread fingers; but the dumpling was the best of all.

It was Grandpa, of course, who had suggested it. "What's a birthday without a dumpling? We always had one in my young days. It's an old Scottish custom. Go on, Janet woman; you make one, and we'll put some wee odds and ends in it."

The wee odds and ends were small trinkets, wrapped up in greaseproof paper and mixed with the currants, raisins and candied peel. There was a small ring and a bell and a thimble and a button. The great thing was to cut the dumpling into slices, and find out who had won a lucky charm.

Wee Maisie Murphy sat in the place of honour with her presents piled in front of her. It was *her* birthday, though she had no idea how old she was. "Theven, I think! Or perhapth eight! I'm ever tho old!"

The Murphies themselves never bothered about birthdays. There were too many of them for that; but Maisie had taken care to remind Macpherson. "Tho that you'll know!" she had said innocently.

It came as no surprise to her when he called to invite her to tea. "Oh yeth! I'm ready!" she cried, and so she was! Maisie was dressed up in all the finery she could find. She was even wearing an old pair of fur gloves and carrying a parasol, though she had only to go one floor up.

They had been here for over a week, but it still felt strange to think of the skyscraper as home. Aunt Janet declared she would never-never-never get used to it. Never! She refused to look out of the window. "No, no! It makes me dizzy!" As for the lifts, "I don't trust them!" she sniffed. "They'll stick one day, mark my words!" All the same, though she would not admit it, she liked her clean new kitchen, and all the gadgets that made housework so easy.

The homeliest touch of all was that the

Murphies lived on the floor below. Never mind how noisy they were! Never mind how often Mrs Murphy came up to borrow tea or sugar, or that Maisie was always ringing the bell and asking for "Macpherthon!" They needed such familiar sounds to offset the strangeness of their new world.

Grandpa, too, gave them a sense of security. The old man had settled in best of all. Not a word of complaint! "What would I complain about?" he grinned. "I've got my chair and my pipe and my ships and Joey and the view!"

Grandpa was enchanted with the view. "Man, Macpherson, it's like being up in an aeroplane!" he cried, gazing at the scene stretched out beneath him. The sight of the River Clyde winding its way past the shipyards delighted him beyond words. "I could look at it for ever and ever!"

Joey, too, had settled down in his cage by the window—and not always in his cage. Now and again Grandpa let him out to stretch his wings. The budgerigar would perch on the old man's finger, and then fly off to land on the mantelpiece, or even on Aunt Janet's shoulder.

"That beast!" she would complain; but Macpherson knew by the flushed look on her cheeks that she liked it, especially when the budgie gave

her a little peck and said, "Hullo, Janet woman!" as if he knew.

Today Joey was pecking the crumbs from Grandpa's plate, waiting for his share of birthday dumpling which Aunt Janet was about to cut.

"I thay! I'm ever tho lucky!" said Maisie, looking for the hundredth time at the presents in front of her. They were small "mindings": a string of coloured beads from Macpherson, a red beret from Aunt Janet, and a pair of real "pearl" earrings from Grandpa. The biggest and most expensive of the presents bore a label: FROM AN ADMIRER.

"What'th an admirer?" Maisie had asked, as she opened the parcel to reveal the biggest box of chocolates she had ever seen, tied up in bows of pink ribbon. "Merthy me! It'll take *dayth* to eat them! I bet they're from Hith Nibth!"

"How would *he* know about your birthday?" asked Macpherson in a grumpy voice. His Nibs had been Maisie's slave ever since the moment she started ordering him about. Not that Macpherson was jealous, of course!

"I wonder?" said Maisie, with an innocent look on her face. She sampled one of the chocolates there and then. "They're great! But I like *your* prethent betht, Macpherthon! Ithn't it time for the dumpling?"

Maisie was delighted to find the ring in her portion. "Ithn't it lucky?" she cried, putting it on her little finger. "It fitth my pinkie!"

Grandpa had found the thimble in *his* helping when the doorbell rang—the sharp trill that was becoming familiar to them by now.

"If that's His Nibs, I'll throttle him!" said Macpherson, going to the door with the light of battle in his eyes. But it was not His Nibs. It was Ching, with an anxious look on his face.

"Master velly ill! Wants to see you!" he said.

"What's wrong?" asked Macpherson, in alarm.

"Fed up!" said Ching, rolling his eyes.

"What?" cried Macpherson. "Is that all?"

"No, no! Not all! Twisted ankle! Not walk! Velly solly for himself! Wants to see you!"

"Huh!" scoffed Macpherson. His Nibs was always feeling sorry for himself. Why should *he* care?

"You'd better go, Macpherson," called Grandpa. "Perhaps the poor boy's really ill."

"Huh!" said Macpherson again. The poor boy, indeed!

"Wait for me, Macpherthon! I'm coming with you!" said Maisie, gathering up her trophies and placing her new red beret on her head. "I'll take Hith Nibth a bit of my dumpling."

Macpherson sat and sulked beside her as the car sped smoothly through the streets. Maisie waved to everybody as if she were the Queen. The open box of chocolates lay on her lap. Now and again she stuffed another in her mouth.

"You'll be sick!" said Macpherson, crossly.

"Yeth! Tho I will! Help yourthelf, Macpherthon!"

They found His Nibs lying on a sofa, with books and toys strewn all around him. His face lit up when he saw his visitors.

"Thank goodness you've come!" he cried, sitting up. "You don't know how bored I've been! It was all Ching's fault! He *will* polish the floor in the hall. I slipped on the rug and twisted my ankle. The doctor says I've not to move for days and days—and I haven't even got my budgie to keep me company." He lay back again, full of self-pity.

Macpherson made a practical suggestion. "Why not buy a new one?"

"No! it wouldn't be the same. I want my own Joey," said His Nibs stubbornly. "I've advertised again and again."

"Here'th a bit of dumpling," said Maisie, to console him. "Oh, and thankth for the thweeth. They're great! Merthy me! What a lot of toyth you've got!"

"I'm tired of them all!" said the boy, peevishly.

"You're a thilly thing!" Maisie scolded him. "You've got everything!"

"I have not! Nothing ever happens to me—except that I go and hurt my ankle. I don't like this dumpling-thing," he said, pushing it away. "I want. . . ."

What he wanted was drowned out by the musical chimes of the doorbell. "Ching! The door!" he called.

"Yes, master! I go!"

Maisie sat down on the floor and began to play with the train. "Perhapth it'th your budgie," she began; but His Nibs silenced her.

"Quiet! Listen! It's my Dad! He's come home!"

A loud booming voice was heard in the hall, followed by the clatter of luggage being dropped on the floor. Then in marched General Biggs-Brown, with as much noise as if he had been a whole army rolled into one.

"Stand to attention, Barnaby, my boy!"

"Can't, Dad! I've hurt my ankle! Oh my! I'm glad to see you home!"

Tears began to shine in his eyes and trickle down his cheeks. At the sight of them, the General forgot his military bearing and strode across the room to clasp his small son in his arms.

"What's this? A bell! Bless my soul! Are you trying to poison me? I might have swallowed it!"

The General was drinking cup after cup of strong tea and eating the dumpling his son had scorned. They were all sitting at his feet listening to his stories and watching every movement he made. He seemed a giant of a man, with great moustaches that twirled up at the ends.

"It'th a charm," explained Maisie. "Today'th my birthday!"

"Really?" The General wiped the little bell and put it away in his pocket. "In that case, I'll keep it for luck. Have you had many presents?"

"Hundredth!" said Maisie lavishly. She began to list them in great detail, while Macpherson tried his best to stop her. At last he grabbed her by the arm and said, "Come on, Maisie! It's time we went home." He had a feeling that father and son ought to be left alone together.

"No, no! Stay for a while and tell me about yourself," boomed the General. "You've been so kind to my boy, keeping him company while I've been away."

Macpherson glanced guiltily at His Nibs, knowing that he had been anything but kind. Now the tables were turned. It was His Nibs who was jealous!

"Keep off!" His eyes seemed to be flashing a message. "He's *my* Dad, not yours!"

"I—I think it's time we went away," said Macpherson uneasily.

"Not till you've told me about that skyscraper of yours," insisted the General, pouring himself another cup of tea. "I've always wondered what it would be like to live in one."

"It'th great!" said Maisie, swallowing another of her chocolates. "You can thee ever tho far—all round the world. It'th perfect!"

Macpherson would have agreed, if Grandpa had not brought him up so strictly to tell the truth. "It's not quite perfect," he told the General. "For one thing, there's no place to play."

Macpherson had not much time to play himself, but he could see what was missing. There was no back-court where the children could run about and let off steam. On wet days they played noisily in the concrete entrance hall, or on the landings between the different floors. Sometimes they took the lifts up and down, while the housewives waited for them in vain, with their laden shopping-baskets.

The General twirled his moustaches as he listened. Once started, Macpherson went on to tell him about Grandpa, and about old Skinflint and the Tarzan Gang; but it was the lack of playing space that seemed to interest his listener most.

"I know!" he boomed out suddenly. "An Adventure Playground! That's the answer! I believe there are some in Glasgow already, but not in your district. I'll see to it!"

If General Biggs-Brown said he would see to something it was as good as done. He had such an air of authority about him.

"What'th an Adventure Playground?" asked Maisie, choosing yet another chocolate.

"You'll be sick, young lady!" warned the General. "An Adventure Playground? Well, it's a playground where you can have adventures! As simple as that!"

"What kind of adventures?" asked Macpherson, growing interested. It was one of his favourite words—adventure!

"Any kind you like! It's up to you," said the

General. "What we provide—I'm on the Committee, so I know all about it—is an open space with plenty of room to let off steam. Plenty of things to play with, too. Not ordinary toys, you know! Old junk! That's what young people like to mess about with: old bicycles, broken-down motor cars, brick walls to knock down, and ropes to swing on. Plenty of things to break, if they want to, or to build up, if they feel like it. If young people get rid of their high spirits in a natural way, perhaps they won't join silly gangs like those Tarzans you were telling me about."

"Fancy!" said Macpherson, his eyes shining. "It sounds great!" He could see himself swinging on a rope ladder, taking an old car to pieces, or hammering nails into a wooden box without anyone shouting: "Don't do that!" It was a wonderful idea!

"I'll see to it!" said the General in a determined voice. "I have a few weeks to spare before going to Mexico." He turned to his son and laid a hand on his shoulder. "I'm taking you with me, my boy."

His Nibs shot a smug glance in Macpherson's direction. "Mexico!" he said. "What do you think of that, Macpherson?"

"Great!" said Macpherson. Yet he was not really envious. Mexico was only a name on the map. The Adventure Playground sounded more real.

Maisie Murphy gave a little hiccup and said, "I think I'm beginning to feel thick."

"Fresh air! That's what you need," said Macpherson, tugging at her arm. "Come on home, Maisie."

He turned to the General, not sure whether to shake hands with him or attempt a salute. "Goodbye, sir, and thank you!" In a less respectful voice he said to young Barnaby, "Cheerio, you!"

"Are you not going to wait and see what Dad's brought me? I expect he's got heaps of presents in his luggage," said His Nibs, looking smugger than ever.

"No, thanks!" said Macpherson, quickly. "Come on Maisie!"

The hall was full of luggage covered with labels from foreign places. There were boxes, too, no doubt filled with new toys for His Nibs. Macpherson stifled his feeling of envy. It took more than new toys to make someone happy.

As Ching showed them out, an old lady arrived at the door, carrying a bird-cage. "His name's Joey! I saw an advertisement in the paper...."

"I hope it's the right one this time," Macpher

son said as they took the lift down. "How are you feeling now, Maisie?"

"F-fine!" she said bravely. "But I don't think I want to eat any more thweeth!"

Nothing more was heard of the Adventure Playground or His Nibs or the General for over a week. Then one day Aunt Janet said to Macpherson, "You'd better go and bring in the washing. It should be dry by now."

"Where is it?" said Macpherson in surprise.

He had been used to bringing in the washing in the old days. It had been a simple matter of running downstairs to the back-green and unpinning the sheets, shirts and aprons from the line. But where could they put a washing-line in a skyscraper?

"It's up on the roof," said Aunt Janet, handing him a key. "I'm never going up there again, if I can help it. Never! It makes me too dizzy. *You*'ll have to hang out the washing in future."

"Okay, I will, Aunt Janet!" He had never been on the roof-top and was eager to see for himself.

He took the lift up, found the door that led to the roof, unlocked it and stepped into a strange, exciting world. At first he could see nothing but sheets and shirts billowing in the breeze. There were rows and rows of washing-lines, propped up by wooden poles. He could recognise Aunt Janet's from her coloured aprons, Grandpa's shirts, and his own striped pyjamas. Above him the clouds, like a giant's washing, scurried past. He could hear the roar and rumble of the traffic far below, and ran to the side to look down. There was no fear of falling over. He was hedged in on all sides by high glassy walls. Though they were strong, Macpherson was delighted to find he could see through them—and there was plenty to see!

The first thing he noticed was a tiny toy van speeding towards the skyscraper, making a cheeky sound with its horn. Even from this distance Macpherson could see that it was Murphy's travelling shop.

"Yoo-hoo, Mr Murphy!" he called, but the words were swept away with the wind.

He could see Maisie, as small as a doll, running to greet her father. Then he looked further afield, taking in the whole vista of streets, towers, parks, river and hills. He felt like a monarch looking down on his kingdom. All this belonged to him. It was *his* Glasgow.

Suddenly his eye was attracted to some movement nearer at hand. A group of workmen were busy on a piece of waste-ground. A lorry, piled high with junk, arrived on the scene. A military-looking man was in command, with a small boy limping by his side. His Nibs!

Macpherson watched while an old car, several bicycles, prams, tyres, ropes and ladders were unloaded.

"Hooray!" High up on the skyscraper Macpherson raised a cheer. The General had been as good as his word. The Adventure Playground was beginning to take shape.

7

An End and a Beginning

Macpherson could not believe his ears—and no wonder!

"Miss Peacock! Did you hear that?"

They were in the back-shop, opening crates of tinned fruit and sorting them into neat heaps. The strange sound was coming from the front of the shop where Old Skinflint was busy behind the counter.

Miss Peacock cocked her head to listen.

"It can't be!" She gasped.

"It is!"

Old Skinflint was *singing!*

If Miss Peacock had suddenly flown through the ceiling Macpherson could not have been more surprised. *"Pom-pom-pom! Pom-pom-pom!"* There were no words and not much tune about it. The grocer's voice was as rusty as an old nail. All the same, it was a brave attempt, coming from him.

"What on earth's got into him?" asked Miss Peacock, with a startled look on her face.

"Perhaps he's sickening for something," suggested Macpherson.

He tiptoed to the door and peered round at the singer. Old Skinflint was almost hidden from sight by a large pile of groceries on the counter. Every now and then he added another tin or jar or packet to the pile and ticked the item off a long list. Every time he completed the operation he gave voice to another *pom-pom-pom*.

Macpherson's heart sank when he saw the size of the pile. Imagine carrying that lot round! It would need the strength of an elephant!

Old Skinflint had reached the end of the list and was totting up the sum. He seemed well pleased with it, so please that he *pom-pom-pom*-ed even louder, and then called out, "Macpherson!"

Macpherson braced himself. Now for it!

"Yes, Mr McGlashan, sir! I'm here!"

He went forward to the counter, and then gave a start of surprise. The grocer's face was twisted into what looked like a *smile!* Macpherson stared at him in alarm, thinking, "Mercy me! Has he gone off his head?"

"I'll go and fetch my message-basket," he began, anxious to get back to Miss Peacock and tell her the latest.

"Take your time! Take your time!" said the grocer mildly.

"What?" gasped Macpherson. Wonders would never cease! He was dreaming, of course! In another moment he and Old Skinflint would fly off to the moon on a magic carpet!

The grocer gave another crooked smile and actually *beamed* at Macpherson. "It's thanks to you I've got this order. Did you ever see such a big one? Don't worry, Macpherson! *You* won't have to carry it. He's sending his Chinese servant. . . ."

"Oh!" Macpherson began to see the light. "The General!"

"Yes, that's him! General Biggs-Brown—a fine gentleman! Very rich!" The grocer rubbed his hands. "What's more, he's going to send some of his friends to the shop, too. All because of you, he told me." Old Skinflint almost chuckled. "That's just what I need. Fashionable customers with plenty of money! Nice big orders!"

Macpherson had never seen him look so pleased. Not that it would last, of course! Wait till the General asked him for some money for the Adventure Playground Fund. *That* would soon wipe the smile from his face!

All the same, Macpherson was thankful for any small mercy. He helped Old Skinflint to pack up the groceries, after which there was one more surprise to come.

"A little present," said Mr McGlashan, searching on the shelves. "You deserve a reward, eh, Macpherson?"

"Well—er—that's very kind of you, Mr McGlashan, sir!"

The grocer picked up a large tin of mixed biscuits. Just the thing to take home to Aunt Janet to keep in her new cupboard! Macpherson was reaching out to accept it when Old Skinflint changed his mind. He put the box back on the shelf and looked around for something less expensive.

"I tell you what, there are some damaged apples in that barrel. Help yourself!" The smile had faded from his face by now at the thought of giving something away for nothing. "Not too many, mind!" he warned.

"No! Okay! Thanks, Mr McGlashan, sir!" said Macpherson, putting a good face on it. He might have known not to expect miracles!

By the end of the day Old Skinflint was back to normal. No more smiles! No more *pom-pom-poms!* His parting words to Macpherson were as sharp as ever. "If you're not in time tomorrow, I'll flay you alive! No dawdling! Do you hear me?"

"Yes, I hear you, Mr McGlashan, sir!"

On the way home a great piece of luck

happened to Macpherson. He was speeding down the street, carrying his bag of damaged apples, when he almost tripped over something lying on the pavement. A purse! He picked it up and looked around for its owner. No one in sight!

"I'd better take it to the Highland bobby," he thought, and ran off to the corner where his favourite policeman was on duty. The bobby was talking to a lady, but he turned to look at Macpherson when the boy ran up to him.

"What's up now? Man, Macpherson, are you being chased by a tiger?"

"No! I've found this!"

"My purse!" cried the lady in a delighted voice. "I've just been telling the policeman that I lost it. Oh my! what a piece of luck! Wait! I must give you something!"

"No, no!" protested Macpherson. "It was nothing!"

But the lady insisted. She took some coins from her purse and thrust them into Macpherson's hand. "You go and buy yourself something. I'm very very grateful to you!"

The Highland bobby grinned at him and said, "Man, Macpherson, you're a millionaire!"

So he was! He put the money in his pocket and went off, wondering what to buy. He had a quick look in each shop-window as he passed. A mink

coat for Aunt Janet? A motor-scooter for Grandpa? A diamond brooch for Maisie? A pair of skis for himself?

He was hurrying past a pet shop when his eye was attracted to a budgie swinging in its cage. A budgie with blue stripes!

"Mercy me! I wonder....?"

He stopped and stared through the window. What if this was the right one? Perhaps he should go in and find out. Yes? No?

It was the shopkeeper who helped him to make up his mind. He came to the door and asked, "Is there anything you fancy, sonny?"

Sonny! Macpherson ignored the insult and pointed to the budgie. "Has it got a name?" he asked.

"Sure, it's got a name. It calls itself Joey!"

"Oh!" Macpherson's heart began to beat faster. "Does it talk much?"

"Never stops! Come in, sonny, and hear for yourself!"

There was a great babble of noise inside the shop. Puppies were barking, cats miaowing and birds twittering. There were white mice running round the little treadmills in their cages. There were hamsters and goldfish and tortoises; but Macpherson had eyes only for Joey.

The man lifted the cage from the window and set it on the counter. Joey took one look at Macpherson and said, "Ching! The door! At once! You hear what Joey says! Yes, master! Yes, master! Velly good!"

It was His Nibs's budgie all right.

"Where did you get it?" asked Macpherson.

"Oh! Somebody came in and sold it to me. I've forgotten who. D'you want it, sonny?"

"How—how much is it?" asked Macpherson, fingering the coins in his pocket.

"Fifty pence!"

Macpherson shook his head.

"Too much?" said the man. "How much

could you pay? I'll make a bargain with you, sonny, if you're keen to have the budgie."

Macpherson had a quick tussle with himself. Why should he waste his precious money on a spoilt child like His Nibs? It would be better fun to spend it on himself. Or, would it? He knew in his heart that this was a chance to clear his conscience and get rid of the silly jealousy he felt every time he met young Barnaby.

"Would you take thirty pence?" he asked the man, bringing the money from his pocket.

"Done! Thirty p. it is! Wait and I'll find a wee box for the budgie. You've got a bargain, sonny!"

Macpherson ran all the way to Carlton Mansions, with Joey chirping, "Yes, master! No, master! Tweet-tweet! Ching! Ching! Ching!"

The porter who looked like an admiral was standing at ease in the hall. Macpherson had to wait for a moment to get his breath back. Then he looked up at the man and said, "Will you do something for me, please?"

"Depends!" said the man, cautiously. "What is it?"

"Will you give this box to His Nibs, and don't tell him who brought it?"

"Okay! Mum's the word!" said the man, taking the box from him.

"Thanks very much," said Macpherson, wondering how to reward him. He fumbled in the bag of apples. "Would you like one? It's only a wee bit damaged."

He left the Admiral turning the apple round and round in his hand, looking for an undamaged bite, and hurried away, feeling as if he had completed a task. That was that! Strangely enough, now that the deed was done, he felt almost fond of His Nibs. In future, when they met, he would try not to be so touchy. Who knew? he and young Barnaby might even become real friends!

In his haste to get home and tell Grandpa, Macpherson forgot that he no longer lived at Number Five Clyde-View Tenements. Without thinking, he ran down the familiar street. Then he suddenly drew up when he heard a shout.

"Look out!"

Crash!

Macpherson leapt back and ducked his head just in time. Before his eyes a whole building came toppling down—roofs, chimneys, walls, ceilings—all were reduced to a heap of rubble. When the dust settled, he saw the gap where his old home had once stood.

He stood there with the dust in his eyes and a lump in his throat, thankful for one thing.

Grandpa was not here to see the ruins. Macpherson could recognise some familiar objects. Surely that was the faded wallpaper from his own little bedroom! Was that the old mantelpiece where Grandpa used to place his ships-in-bottles? Beside it lay the broken cupboard where Aunt Janet once kept her pots of jam and cups and saucers; and he could see, too, the door of the coal-cellar—his old hiding-place—smashed to pieces.

Macpherson was rubbing the dust, and a few tears, from his eyes when he heard a cheerful *toot-toot* from behind. He turned round to see Murphy's travelling shop drawing up with a skid.

"Jump in, me boyo, and I'll drive you home," cried Murphy, leaning out and opening the door. He took one quick look at the debris and said, "Bedad! I'm not going to watch! No use crying over spilt milk. It's over and done with. Besides, I'm getting quite fond of me skyscraper. Sure, it's not the place that matters; it's the people who live there. Hang on to your hat, Macpherson, me darlin', I'm going to turn me van round!"

Murphy whirled the van round in a circle, then went jogging forward like a bucking bronco, leaving a cloud of dust in his wake.

Macpherson sat beside him with a set look on his face. "No, no! Don't look back!" he told himself. "Look forward!" Forward into the future.

Straight ahead he saw it waiting for him—the upright giant that was now his home. He looked up-up-up to the twenty-second floor. Was that Grandpa at the window, talking to Joey in his cage?

"Yoo-hoo, Grandpa! Look down!"

The old man could not hear him,. but he looked down, all the same, and gave a cheerful wave. At the sight of it Macpherson felt a warm glow inside him. It was a mixed-up world, right enough, full of good things and bad. Who knew what was round the next corner? But that was what made life so exciting—like an Adventure Playground!

"Hold on, Grandpa! I'm coming up!" he cried, smiling and waving.

f you have enjoyed this book, here are some others :hat you might like to read, also published by <nnight Books:

KNIGHT BOOKS

MACPHERSON'S ISLAND

Lavinia Derwent

Grandpa has been ill and the nurse says he must have a holiday if he's to get better. Macpherson is very worried – they can't possibly afford a holiday and anyway, his miserly boss, Old Skinflint, would never let him leave the shop. But help comes unexpectedly from quiet Miss Peacock, and in no time at all she's actually persuaded Old Skinflint to drive Macpherson and Grandpa (and Maisie Murphy!) to Seagull Island to stay with her sister.

And what an adventurous holiday it turns out to be!

KNIGHT BOOKS

MACPHERSON'S LIGHTHOUSE ADVENTURE

Lavinia Derwent

Things are always happening to Macpherson, the young errand boy who lives in the city with his old seadog of a grandfather and his crotchety Aunt Janet. Now they're all off to the seaside for a fortnight's free holiday – and, of course, there are plenty of adventures in store there for Macpherson.

There's the time Macpherson and Grandpa almost capsize in their oary-boat, thanks to the reckless Lord Roland, and when Macpherson joins the lifeboat crew to rescue a wrecked fishing boat. But most exciting of all is his adventure at the lighthouse . . . It's certainly an eventful holiday for Macpherson!

KNIGHT BOOKS

ME!

Gyles Brandreth

ME! is a book all about YOU!

It asks you hundreds of questions about yourself and provides you with spaces to fill in the answers. Once you have completed the book it will be a unique guide to everything there is to know about you.

There has never been a book quite like this one before!

KNIGHT BOOKS

THE CLUE-CRACKER'S CROSSWORD BOOK

R. S. Philpott

Test your general knowledge and word power with this entertaining, brain-teasing crossword book. It's packed with puzzles on a variety of subjects. LIVING CREATURES, WAR, FIRST NAMES and SPORT are just some of them.

KNIGHT BOOKS

E. NESBIT FAIRY STORIES

EDITED AND WITH AN INTRODUCTION BY
NAOMI LEWIS
ILLUSTRATED BY BRIAN ROBB

E. Nesbit's timeless stories – amongst them THE RAILWAY CHILDREN and THE PHOENIX AND THE CARPET – have been loved by children for many years, and today are equally popular on television and film.

This is an enchanting collection of her original fairy stories, full of the unique Nesbit blend of ingenious invention, everyday logic, magic and special humour.

KNIGHT BOOKS

BOBBY BREWSTER

H. E. TODD

Bobby Brewster is just an ordinary small boy, but it is surprising how everyday events always seem to take a magical turn when he's around.

H. E. Todd is a renowned storyteller who has made many appearances on television, particularly BBC's Jackanory, and has held storytelling sessions all over the world.

Bobby Brewster titles published by Knight Books:

BOBBY BREWSTER'S TORCH
BOBBY BREWSTER'S SCARECROW
BOBBY BREWSTER'S DETECTIVE
BOBBY BREWSTER'S GHOST
BOBBY BREWSTER'S TYPEWRITER
BOBBY BREWSTER'S FIRST FUN
BOBBY BREWSTER'S WALLPAPER
BOBBY BREWSTER'S CONKER
BOBBY BREWSTER'S POTATO

KNIGHT BOOKS

ENID BLYTON'S RUBY STORYBOOK
ENID BLYTON'S EMERALD STORYBOOK

Enid Blyton is one of the best-loved children's authors of all time. This is a new edition of a collection of her stories for younger children, delightfully illustrated throughout by Angie Sage. While the stories are an ideal length for reading aloud, the vocabulary is simple enough for the beginning reader to tackle for him or herself.

KNIGHT BOOKS